BUYERS AND SELLERS REAL ESTATE HANDBOOK

1490318
13.98
32%
2

by
Alan Ray Hoxie

Copyright © 1999, 2001 by ALAN RAY HOXIE, BROKER
G.R.I.
All rights reserved.
No part of this book may be reproduced, stored in a retrieval system, or transmitted by any means, electronic, mechanical, photocopying, recording, or otherwise, without written permission from the author.

ISBN: 0-75962-865-3

This book is printed on acid free paper.

1stBooks – rev. 6/13/01

DEDICATION

TO MY MOM, SHIRLEY

MY WIFE, CHRIS

and MARY FREEDMAN, who typed this thing and helped revise it 5 times.

PREFACE

ALAN HOXIE IS A REAL ESTATE BROKER IN SYRACUSE, NEW YORK, AND OWNS HOXIE REAL ESTATE. HE ALSO HOLDS A G.R.I. DESIGNATION, ONE OF THE HIGHEST IN RESIDENTIAL REAL ESTATE. ALAN HAS BEEN IN THE REAL ESTATE BUSINESS FOR 15 YEARS AND HAS SOLD OVER $10 MILLION IN PROPERTY. HE WAS THE SUPERVISOR OF THE TOWN OF ONONDAGA, A TOWN OF 20,000 RESIDENTS, BORDERING SYRACUSE. ALAN IS A 1972 GRADUATE OF LEMOYNE COLLEGE. HE HAS TWICE BEEN PRESIDENT OF THE SOUTH SIDE BUSINESS ASSOCIATION IN SYRACUSE.

ALAN IS A REGULAR CONTRIBUTOR TO THE LOCAL CHAMBER OF COMMERCE AS A SPEAKER, AND HE HAS WRITTEN A REAL ESTATE COLUMN FOR A WEEKLY SYRACUSE NEWSPAPER. ALAN HAS BEEN ON THE LEGISLATIVE AND EDUCATION COMMITTEE FOR THE GREATER SYRACUSE BOARD OF REALTORS. HE ALSO TEACHES THE REAL ESTATE SALESPERSON QUALIFYING COURSE. HE IS AN INSTRUCTOR,

CERTIFIED AND APPROVED BY NEW YORK STATE, FOR THESE COURSES AND THE HOME INSPECTOR COURSE.

HE IS CURRENTLY EMPLOYED BY NEW YORK STATE IN THE DIVISION OF HOUSING AND COMMUNITY RENEWAL, AS A CAPITAL PROJECTS MANAGER.

TABLE OF CONTENTS

1. BUYING A SINGLE FAMILY HOME 1
2. SELLING YOUR HOME 18
3. FOR SALE BY OWNER 29
4. NOTHING DOWN, NOTHING DOING 36
5. BUYING INVESTMENT PROPERTY DEALING WITH TENANT'S AND EVICTIONS, RENT PROGRAMS WHERE THE DEALS ARE 54
6. BUYING AND DEVELOPING LAND AN OVERVIEW 66
7. NEW CONSTRUCTION (BUYING YOUR NEW HOME) 75
8. MORTGAGES 81
9. AUCTIONS 102
10. GRIEVING YOUR ASSESSMENT (PROPERTY TAXES) 110
11. NEGOTIATING - GETTING YOUR THOUGHTS ACROSS 116
12. C O N C L U S I O N 145

INTRODUCTION

WELCOME. THIS BOOK WILL HELP YOU ON YOUR WAY TO OWNING REAL ESTATE AND PERHAPS OWNING IT TO THE EXTENT THAT YOUR INCOME MAY BE GREATLY ENHANCED BY YOUR PRUDENT REAL ESTATE ACTIVITY.

THIS BOOK SERVES TO ENLIGHTEN YOU ABOUT THE PITFALLS OF ALL THE "NOTHING DOWN" SEMINARS AND SHOWS WE SEE ON T.V. IF MAKING A FORTUNE IN REAL ESTATE WAS AS EASY AS THE PEOPLE ON T.V. SAY IT IS, WHY ARE THEY SELLING TAPES AND NOT LOOKING FOR THAT NEXT BIG DEAL? I WILL REVIEW IN DETAIL SOME OF THE WAYS TO ACQUIRE PROPERTY WITHOUT A GREAT DEAL OF MONEY. SOME I HAVE DONE MYSELF. SO BEFORE YOU TAKE OUT THAT CREDIT CARD AND GO FOR THE PHONE, READ THIS BOOK AND SAVE YOURSELF A BUNDLE OF MONEY.

WE ALSO DISCUSS BUYING AND SELLING YOUR FIRST HOME IN AN ATTEMPT TO GIVE YOU A HEAD START WHEN YOU ENTER THE INCREASINGLY COMPETITIVE REAL ESTATE MARKET AS EITHER A BUYER WHO WANTS TO "BUY IT RIGHT" OR A SELLER

WHO WANTS TO "SELL IT QUICK." IN EITHER CASE, THE MORE EDUCATED YOU BECOME, THE LESS NEED FOR A REAL ESTATE PROFESSIONAL. THEY SEE THE HANDWRITING ON THE WALL. DO YOU? MR HOXIE CAN BE REACHED AT   ahoxie@twcny.rr.com

ALAN HOXIE, BROKER, G.R.I.

BUYING A SINGLE FAMILY HOME

BEFORE ACTUALLY GOING OUT INTO THE WORLD TO LOOK FOR THAT DREAM HOME, THERE ARE MANY THINGS THAT YOU, THE POTENTIAL BUYER, SHOULD DO TO MINIMIZE THE NEGATIVE EFFECTS OF THIS TRULY AMERICAN EXPERIENCE.

IN REAL ESTATE, WE OFTEN HEAR HORROR STORIES FROM BUYERS WHO HAVE ANY NUMBER OF TALES TO TELL ABOUT THE DRUDGERY OF HOME BUYING. THEY BLAME THEIR BUYING MISERY ON REAL ESTATE AGENTS, LAWYERS, BANKS, SELLERS, THE ECONOMY, THEIR RELATIVES, ETC. THE TRUTH OF THE MATTER, HOWEVER, IS THAT MOST OF THEIR PROBLEM WAS CAUSED BY THEIR OWN LACK OF PERSONAL RESEARCH BEFORE THEY JUMPED INTO THAT BUYER STREAM. FIRST, YOU MUST DECIDE WHAT TYPE OF HOUSE YOU DON'T WANT. "I COULD NEVER LIVE IN A RANCH STYLE HOME." YOU SAY, "THAT'S FINE, WE'LL LOOK AT COLONIALS." IT'S IMPORTANT TO NARROW DOWN THE STYLE OF HOUSE AND ITS AMENITIES. DO YOU WANT A 2 CAR GARAGE, 1 - 1/2 BATHS OR 2- 1/2 BATHS? WOULD YOU PREFER A FINISHED BASEMENT?

ONCE YOU HAVE THE STYLE NARROWED DOWN DEPENDING ON YOUR LIFE PLANS, YOU SHOULD GO TO A MORTGAGE COMPANY OR A BANK AND FIND OUT JUST HOW MUCH OF A MORTGAGE YOU ARE QUALIFIED FOR AND THE CONDITION OF YOUR CREDIT.

I HAVE SHOWED COUNTLESS HOMES TO BUYERS WHO I LATER DISCOVERED HAD TERRIBLE CREDIT, EVEN THOUGH I MADE IT A POINT RIGHT IN THE BEGINNING TO ASK ABOUT THEIR CREDIT. THE BANK WILL ULTIMATELY FIND OUT ABOUT YOUR INCOME, CREDIT, JUDGMENTS, ETC. THERE ARE MANY FINANCING PLANS AVAILABLE AND MANY CREDIT BLEMISHES ARE ACCEPTABLE BY LENDING INSTITUTIONS. SO BE HONEST AND START FROM A SOLID FOUNDATION.

THE AMOUNT YOU CAN FINANCE WILL DETERMINE WHETHER YOU CAN SAFELY PURSUE LOOKING AT NEW CONSTRUCTION OR A LESS EXPENSIVE RESALE HOME.

THE NEXT STEP AND, BY THE WAY, WE HAVEN'T EVEN LEFT OUR LIVING ROOM YET, IS TO NARROW DOWN WHAT SPECIFIC AREA OF THE COUNTY WE WOULD LIKE TO LIVE IN. MANY FACTORS HAVE TO

BE CONSIDERED HERE AND, AGAIN, THE PRICE OF HOMES IN CERTAIN AREAS WILL BE A DECIDING FACTOR. YOU HAVE TO CONSIDER TRAFFIC FLOW. DO YOU WANT TO PUT UP WITH A DAILY TRAFFIC JAM IN EITHER DIRECTION ON YOUR WAY TO AND FROM WORK? IF YOU HAVE CHILDREN, WHAT IS THE SCHOOL SYSTEM LIKE? HOW MUCH ARE AVERAGE PROPERTY TAXES, WHICH VARY FROM TOWN TO TOWN? DOES YOUR SPOUSE WANT TO BE CLOSE TO FAMILY? BELIEVE IT OR NOT, THAT IS AN OVERRIDING CONCERN FOR SOME.

YOU CAN ASSIST YOUR REAL ESTATE AGENT OR YOURSELF, IF YOU DECIDE TO GO IT ALONE, BY NARROWING DOWN THE AREA AS MUCH AS POSSIBLE. IT IS PROBABLY TO YOUR BENEFIT TO USE A REAL ESTATE AGENT SINCE THEY HAVE ACCESS TO THE M.L.S. SYSTEM AND YOU CAN PREVIEW MORE HOMES MORE QUICKLY. ALTHOUGH AFTER READING THIS BOOK, YOU WILL BE MORE QUALIFIED TO SHOP, MOST "FOR SALE BY OWNER" PROPERTIES ARE OVERPRICED AND, WITHOUT SUFFICIENT COMPARISON, YOU MAY NOT GET A GOOD DEAL AT ALL BUYING A FOR SALE BY OWNER PROPERTY. THE, "GREED FACTOR" IN THIS GROUP IS HIGHER THAN IN MOST LISTED SELLERS,

AND NOT ONLY DO THEY NOT WANT TO PAY THE COMMISSION, THEY USUALLY WANT A PREMIUM FOR THEIR HOME WHICH, OF COURSE, IS THE "BEST ON THE BLOCK."

NOW YOU HAVE THE STYLE HOUSE NARROWED DOWN, THE AREAS, AND KNOW YOUR PRICE RANGE. BY NOW, YOU HAVE HAD YOUR CREDIT CHECKED BY A LENDING INSTITUTION, AND YOU ARE READY TO LOOK FOR A REALTOR TO HELP YOU FIND THAT RIGHT PROPERTY.

SINCE EVERYBODY AND THEIR MOTHER HAS A REAL ESTATE LICENSE SOMEWHERE IN THE FAMILY, HOW DO YOU CHOOSE SOMEONE TO WORK WITH? I GET MOST OF MY BUSINESS FROM REFERRALS AND OPEN HOUSES ON PROPERTY I'VE LISTED. THE PRIMARY REASONS FOR REALTORS HOLDING OPEN HOUSES IS (I) TO OBTAIN CUSTOMERS FOR FUTURE SALES AND (2) TO CONVINCE THE SELLER YOU'RE TRYING TO SELL THE HOME (HOWEVER, IF IT WASN'T SO OVERPRICED, YOU WOULDN'T HAVE TO HOLD IT OPEN TO SELL IT). I WOULD FIRST LOOK FOR AN AGENT WITH SOME KIND OF ADVANCED REAL ESTATE DESIGNATION, BROKER, G.R.I., C.R.S., OR C.R.B. THESE DESIGNATIONS SHOW THAT THE AGENT

CARES ENOUGH ABOUT REAL ESTATE AS A CAREER TO LEARN AS MUCH AS POSSIBLE ABOUT THE BUSINESS. YOU WILL ALSO WANT TO WORK WITH SOMEONE FAMILIAR WITH THE AREA WHO WILL KNOW WHETHER THE HOME YOU EVENTUALLY DESIRE IS PRICED RIGHT. THE BEST WAY TO FIND A REALTOR IS BY GOING TO OPEN HOUSES AND SIMPLY TELLING THE AGENT WHAT YOU ARE LOOKING FOR. THERE IS NOTHING WRONG WITH DOING THIS ON THREE OR FOUR OCCASIONS. YOU MAY, HOWEVER, FIND AN AGENT WHOSE PERSONALITY CLICKS WITH YOURS AND YOU HIT IT OFF WELL. BEWARE OF THE AGENT WHO TRIES TO BE TOO PUSHY. SOME COMPANIES TELL THEIR AGENTS THAT THEY ARE TO SHOW NO MORE THAN TEN HOUSES AND THEN CLOSE A SALE. AS A BUYER, THIS MUST BE FRIGHTENING NEWS, BUT AS REAL ESTATE AGENT WHOSE LIVELIHOOD DEPENDS SOLELY ON COMMISSION, IT IS THE ONLY WAY TO ELIMINATE THE TIRE KICKERS. DON'T BE PRESSURED, AND DON'T BE OVERWHELMED. BUYING A HOUSE IS NOT, AS MOST SAY, THE BIGGEST INVESTMENT IN YOUR LIFE SINCE, IN MOST CASES, THE BANK WILL OWN 75-95% OF YOUR HOME. THEY TAKE A BIGGER RISK THAN YOU

DO. YOUR BIGGEST INVESTMENT IS MARRIAGE; THE SECOND IS THE HOUSE.

AFTER YOU'VE SEEN ABOUT A DOZEN HOMES, I BELIEVE YOU ARE READY TO START WRITING OFFERS. YOU MAY PUT IN TWO OR THREE OFFERS ON VARIOUS PROPERTIES UNTIL A DEAL IS STRUCK. DON'T HESITATE BUYING PROPERTY BECAUSE OF FEAR. IF YOU BREAK DOWN YOUR EFFORTS LOGICALLY: (I) YOU WANT A HOME OR HAVE BEEN TOLD BY YOUR ACCOUNTANT TO BUY A HOME. (2) YOU ARE LOOKING FOR A HOME. (3) BUY A HOME AND BE DONE WITH IT. DON'T LET PEOPLE TALK YOU INTO NOT BUYING. IT'S NOT A GOOD TIME, INTEREST RATES ARE TOO HIGH, I'LL WAIT UNTIL I HAVE MORE MONEY SAVED - ARE SOME COMMON EXCUSES. STUDIES SHOW THAT AN INDIVIDUAL WON'T HAVE ANY MORE SPENDABLE INCOME NEXT YEAR THAN HE DOES NOW, SO GO FOR IT.

SHOULD YOUR AGENT BE FROM A LARGE COMPANY~ REAL ESTATE AGENTS ARE USUALLY INDEPENDENT CONTRACTORS, WORKING FOR THEMSELVES. SOME OF THE BUSIER AGENTS MAY NOT HAVE TIME FOR YOU, DEPENDING ON YOUR PRICE RANGE AND THE AREA YOU DESIRE. GO WITH

THE AGENT WHO SEEMS TO CALL YOU THE MOST WITH DRIVE-BY INFORMATION AND WHO SETS UP APPOINTMENTS FOR YOU TO SEE HOUSES. A DRIVE-BY IS A GOOD IDEA FOR YOU TO INITIALLY SEE THE NEIGHBORHOOD, BUT HAVING PASSED THAT TEST, YOU MUST GO IN TO SEE THE HOME. DON'T FEEL THAT YOU ARE INCONVENIENCING THE SELLERS BY WANTING TO SEE THE HOME AT HOURS CONVENIENT TO YOU. THEY WANT TO SELL, AND THEY SHOULD EXPECT SOME INCONVENIENCE.

I THINK THAT WE SHOULD BACK UP A LITTLE TO EXPLAIN A PREVIOUS PARAGRAPH. I SAID THAT AN AGENT MAY NOT WANT TO WORK WITH YOU, DEPENDING ON YOUR PRICE RANGE AND AREA. IF AN AGENT HAS TEN PROSPECTS, ALL LOOKING AT $150,000 HOMES, YOU ARE NOT GOING TO GET THE ATTENTION FROM THAT AGENT IF YOUR RANGE IS IN THE 70's. REMEMBER THAT AND WORK WITH SOMEONE WHO WILL TAKE THE TIME TO SHOW YOU WHAT YOU WANT, AND THIS IS PURELY A PERSONAL DECISION. SOME PEOPLE LIKE TO BE PUSHED, SOME LED, SOME ADVISED, AND SOME MOTHERED. THIS ALL DEPENDS ON YOUR PERSONAL DEGREE OF REAL ESTATE KNOWLEDGE AND AWARENESS.

Alan Ray Hoxie

AS FAR AS THE SIZE OF THE COMPANY GOES, I HAVE WORKED FOR SMALL COMPANIES, FOR MYSELF, AND FOR A LARGE FRANCHISE. AS A BUYER, IT PROBABLY IS NOT AS CRITICAL TO WORK WITH AN AGENT FROM A LARGE FIRM AS IT IS FOR THE SELLER TO LIST THE HOME WITH A LARGE COMPANY. AN AGENT FROM A SMALL COMPANY IN AN M.L.S. SYSTEM CAN SHOW ANY HOME LISTED WITH ANY COMPANY. FROM THE SELLERS PROSPECTIVE, A LARGER FIRM HAS MORE MONEY TO ADVERTISE THE HOME, CAN DO IT MORE FREQUENTLY, HAS A GLOSSIER, MORE PROFESSIONAL PRESENTATION PACKAGE, AND CAN DO THE THINGS THAT WILL MAKE THE HOME SELL FOR THE MOST MONEY POSSIBLE IN THE SHORTEST PERIOD OF TIME.

ONCE YOU HAVE SEEN A DOZEN OR SO HOUSES IN THE AREAS YOU'VE CHOSEN , YOU'LL BEGIN TO HAVE A FEELING FOR COMPARABLE PRICES. WHEN YOU DECIDE TO PUT AN OFFER IN ON THAT HOME THAT STANDS OUT ABOVE THE OTHERS, DON'T BE AFRAID TO COME IN LOW TO TEST THE WATERS, ESPECIALLY IN A BUYER'S MARKET. IF THE HOUSE HAS BEEN ON THE MARKET A LONG TIME, TEST THE WATERS; IF THE HOUSE IS SUBSTANTIALLY ABOVE THE PRICE OF

THOSE IN THE AREA, TEST THE WATERS; IF THE HOUSE NEEDS OBVIOUS REPAIR OR RENOVATION OR REDECORATING, TEST THE WATERS.

IF THE HOME IS IN SUPER CONDITION, IS NEWLY ON THE MARKET, AND IS PRICED AT OR BELOW COMPARABLE PROPERTIES IN THE NEIGHBORHOOD, YOU MAY LOSE THE HOME BY INSISTING ON SUBMITTING A "LOW BALL" OFFER IF YOU WRITE UP AN OFFER FOR $72,000 AND THE HOME IS ON THE MARKET FOR $78,000 AND YOUR AGENT CALLS YOU IN A PANIC AND SAYS, "I'M SUPPOSED TO PRESENT YOUR OFFER AT 7 P.M. TONIGHT, BUT SINCE THEN, I'VE HEARD THERE WILL BE TWO OTHER OFFERS, WHAT DO YOU WANT TO DO?" YOU HAD BETTER DO SOME SERIOUS SOUL SEARCHING AND DECIDE TO COME UP WITH AN ADDITIONAL $6,000 OVER 30 YEARS TO GET THE HOME, PROVIDING YOU REALLY WANT IT. THE SMALL AMOUNT IN INCREASED MONTHLY PAYMENT SHOULDN'T DISPLACE YOUR HAPPINESS.

HOMES HAVE EMOTIONAL APPEAL AS WELL AS PRACTICAL APPEAL AND MANY PEOPLE FORGET THAT. I FEEL THAT MOST MEN COULD LIVE IN COFFEE CANS AND THAT IT IS THE WOMEN WHO BUY

HOUSES, BUT THIS, OF COURSE, IS ONLY MY OPINION. YOU PUT AN OFFER IN ON A HOUSE BECAUSE YOU FEEL THAT YOU CAN IDENTIFY WITH THE HOUSE AND THE ENTIRE NEIGHBORHOOD. DON'T LET IT SLIP BY OVER A MATTER OF PRINCIPLE INVOLVING A FEW HUNDRED OR EVEN THOUSAND DOLLARS. THE SELLER OF ANYTHING ALWAYS HOLDS THE HAMMER, SO DON'T STAND ON PRINCIPLE OVER A FEW DOLLARS EITHER WAY.

WHEN YOU ARE OUT PREVIEWING HOUSES, THERE ARE CERTAIN THINGS YOU SHOULD ASK ABOUT AND COMPARE. YOU MAY USE THE FOLLOWING PAGE TO INSERT THE INFORMATION IN THE BLANKS.

AGE   CONDITION   TYPE

THE HOUSE IS HOW OLD _____?

1. ROOF

2. PAINT OR SIDING

3. FURNACE

4. HOT WATER TANK

5. SEPTIC TANK

6. PLUMBING

Buyers and Sellers Real Estate Handbook

7. ELECTRICAL _____

       CIRCUIT BREAKER_____FUSES_____AMPS

8. DRIVEWAY

9. POOL FILTER

10. APPLIANCES

11. KITCHEN OR BATH REDECORATING

12. FLOORING

13. DOES THE ROOF OR BASEMENT LEAK OR BACK UP?

14. HAVE YOU HAD FOUNDATION PROBLEMS OR PROBLEMS WITH INSECTS?

15. HOW IS THE WATER PRESSURE?

16. WHAT APPLIANCES STAY?

HOW MUCH IS YOUR AVERAGE UTILITY BILL?

WHAT ARE THE TAXES?

DO YOU HAVE ANY EXEMPTIONS?

WHAT DON'T YOU LIKE ABOUT THE HOME, OR WHY ARE YOU MOVING?

   BY FINDING OUT THE ANSWERS TO THESE QUESTIONS, YOU WILL FIND OUT MUCH TO CALM YOUR MIND AND MAKE YOU THINK ABOUT RELATIVE

PRICE. FIND OUT ABOUT UTILITY BILLS. IN NORTHERN CLIMATES, A HOME HEATED BY ELECTRIC HEAT MAY COST SEVERAL HUNDRED DOLLARS PER MONTH IN THE WINTER. THERE IS A HOME THAT HAS ALL ELECTRIC HEAT AROUND THE CORNER FROM MY OFFICE THAT HAS HAD THREE OWNERS IN THREE YEARS AND NOW SITS VACANT. ONE WINTER IS ENOUGH FOR THESE FOLKS WHEN THEY SEE THEIR UTILITY BILL. IT'S TOO BAD BECAUSE IT IS A LOVELY HOME ON A BEAUTIFUL COUNTRY LOT. DON'T BE AFRAID TO ASK THE OWNER WHAT THEY DON'T LIKE ABOUT THE HOME. YOU'D BE SURPRISED AT THE KIND OF INFORMATION YOU'LL FIND OUT. ONE CUSTOMER OF MINE WHO LOVED A HOUSE AND ASKED THAT QUESTION WAS TOLD THAT THE HOUSE WAS FINE BUT THAT HE, THE OWNER, HAD CONTINUALLY ARGUED WITH THE NEIGHBOR WHO REGULARLY PARKED HIS TRACTOR TRAILER IN THE FRONT YARD FOR 26 YEARS. IT WASN'T THERE WHEN WE WENT THROUGH. THAT WAS THE END OF THAT HOME PREVIEW. "WHY ARE YOU MOVING", ANOTHER CUSTOMER ASKED THE SELLER ON OUR WAY THROUGH A GORGEOUS SPLIT LEVEL. "WELL", THE MAN SAID, "I'M TIRED OF BEING AWAKENED BY THE

AMBULANCES EVERY NIGHT." WHAT WE DIDN'T REALIZE WAS THAT HE LIVED ABOUT 1/8 MILE FROM A BUSY INTERSECTION WHICH WAS JUST DOWN THE ROAD FROM A MAJOR HOSPITAL AND THE EMERGENCY VEHICLES CRANKED IT UP JUST BEFORE HIS HOUSE. THAT WAS THE END OF THAT HOME PREVIEW. ALSO, WHEN ASKING WHY PEOPLE ARE MOVING, THEY MAY TELL YOU THEY'RE GETTING DIVORCED.

IN A DIVORCE SITUATION, I HAVE SEEN MANY BUYERS GET EXCELLENT DEALS BECAUSE IN SUCH AN EMOTIONAL SETTING, PRICE SEEMS TO TAKE A BACK SEAT TO MORE IMPORTANT FAMILY MATTERS (CUSTODY, ETC.). THE SAME IS TRUE FOR ESTATES. IN AN ESTATE SITUATION, MANY TIMES THERE ARE SEVERAL OFFSPRING WHO JUST WANT TO BE RID OF A PROPERTY AND GO ON. START LOW ON YOUR OFFER WITH ESTATES, ESPECIALLY IF THEY NEED WORK, AND MANY DO. ELDERLY PEOPLE USUALLY HAVE NOT UPDATED A HOUSE AND WON'T SPEND A PENNY UNTIL SOMETHING BREAKS. LOOK FOR DEALS ON ESTATES, ESPECIALLY IF YOU FLATTER THE ESTATE BY INSERTING A CLAUSE IN YOUR OFFER, "THE BUYER WILL PAY FOR ALL BANK REQUIRED REPAIRS

UP TO $1,000." THIS WASHES THEIR HANDS OF MORE COSTLY WORK IN A HOUSE THEY WISH TO FORGET. USUALLY, THE WORK REQUIRED IS MINOR AND YOU CAN GET MORE PROPORTIONALLY BY ASSUMING THAT RESPONSIBILITY.

SHOULD YOU HIRE AN INSPECTOR? THIS ALL DEPENDS. IF YOU ARE SINKING A GOOD CHUNK OF YOUR OWN MONEY INTO THE HOME AND EITHER IT HAS BEEN VACANT OR LOOKS IN NEED OF REPAIR, THIS PROBABLY IS NOT A BAD IDEA. HOME INSPECTORS, HOWEVER, WILL COST YOU $200 OR MORE FOR THEIR REPORT. RECENTLY, I HAVE BEGUN TEACHING A HOME INSPECTION COURSE FOR ONE OF OUR LOCAL REAL ESTATE SCHOOLS. I HAD NOT REALIZED HOW INFORMED INSPECTORS HAVE TO BE, NOT SPECIFICALLY, BUT IN GENERAL KNOWLEDGE AND BE ABLE TO SPOT A PROBLEM WHEN THEY SEE ONE. A HOME INSPECTOR CAN SPEND THE TIME YOU COULD NOT TO CHECK THE SYSTEMS OF THE HOME FOR PROPER FUNCTIONING. THE INSPECTOR ALMOST ALWAYS GOES THROUGH THE HOME WITH THE BUYER AND POINTS OUT THE PROBLEMS, CLARIFIES THE REMEDY AND WHETHER THE INSPECTOR FEELS THAT IT IS A MINOR OR MORE MAJOR DEFICIENCY. I

HAVE NOT HAD A REAL ESTATE DEAL DESTROYED BY THE FINDINGS OF A HOME INSPECTOR AND, IN FACT, MY CUSTOMERS WERE GLAD THEY HAD ONE DONE. REGARDING A HOME I SOLD LAST YEAR, IT HAD BEEN RENTED FOR A YEAR WHILE STILL ON THE MARKET, BUT WAS VACANT WHEN I SHOWED IT. THE HOME INSPECTOR POINTED OUT SOME MINOR PROBLEMS, BUT INDICATED THAT THE ELECTRICAL SERVICE TO THE HOME OUTSIDE THE HOUSE WAS FRAYED AND WIRING EXPOSED. ADDITIONALLY, THE HOME HAD 60 AMP FUSES, AND HE RECOMMENDED AT LEAST 100 AMP, CIRCUIT BREAKERS. THE HOMEOWNER AGREED TO PAY FOR THIS UPDATE, AND IT SAVED MY CUSTOMER $500 OUT OF HIS OWN POCKET. THERE ARE SEVERAL OTHER CUSTOMERS I HAVE HAD WHERE THIS SAME SCENARIO WAS PLAYED OUT. I AM BECOMING MORE AND MORE IN FAVOR OF A HOME INSPECTION. I BELIEVE IT IS OF VALUE FOR THE MONEY PAID. IN MANY CONTRACTS TO PURCHASE, IT IS STATED THAT THE APPLIANCES, FURNACE, ELECTRICAL SYSTEM, PLUMBING OR HOT WATER TANK HAVE TO BE IN WORKING ORDER WHEN TITLE PASSES. ADDITIONALLY, IN MANY STATES A SELLER'S DISCLOSURE OF PROPERTY CONDITION IS REQUIRED

TO BE COMPLETED HONESTLY AND SIGNED BY THE SELLER, DISCLOSING ANY KNOWN DEFECTS IN THE PROPERTY.

IN HOMES THAT ARE CURRENTLY OCCUPIED, THE MAJOR SYSTEMS ARE PROBABLY FUNCTIONAL SINCE THE FAMILY HAS TO LIVE THERE DAILY. THERE MAY BE, HOWEVER, SIGNS OF WATER LEAKAGE IN THE BASEMENT THAT IS NOT EVIDENT ON A DAILY BASIS BUT ONLY OCCASIONALLY OR SEASONALLY. STILL, EVIDENCE OF PROBLEMS COULD BE LEFT ON BASEMENT WALLS OR TILE FLOORS. FOUNDATION PROBLEMS ARE USUALLY EVIDENT AND MINOR CRACKS ARE NOT UNCOMMON. REMEMBER, BY THE TIME YOU PUT AN OFFER IN ON A HOME, YOU HAVE PROBABLY SEEN IT ONLY TWICE AND MOST LIKELY FOR ONLY FIFTEEN OR TWENTY MINUTES ON EACH WALK THROUGH. AN INSPECTOR WILL SPEND TWO TO THREE HOURS WITH YOU AND TEST AND CHECK APPLIANCES AND SYSTEMS, WHERE POSSIBLE. ROOF AGE AND DECK DETERIORATION ARE HARD TO DETERMINE FROM THE OUTSIDE. IT TAKES SOMEONE TO GET TO THE ATTIC OR CRAWLSPACE WITH AN EYE FOR WHAT TO LOOK FOR. IT IS NOT UNCOMMON FOR IT TO TAKE THREE TO SIX MONTHS TO FIND THE

RIGHT HOME. YOU WILL FEEL MORE COMFORTABLE ABOUT WRITING AN OFFER AFTER YOU'VE BEEN IN THE MARKET MIX FOR A MONTH OR SO AND HAVE BECOME FAMILIAR WITH HOMES PRICED RIGHT AND THOSE "BUILT ON OIL WELLS." YOU'LL BE ABLE TO DEFEND YOURSELF FROM THOSE FOR SALE BY OWNER PROPERTIES.

Alan Ray Hoxie

SELLING YOUR HOME

WHEN IT COMES TIME TO PUT THE OLD HOUSE ON THE MARKET, THE FIRST THING WE NORMALLY THINK OF ARE REAL ESTATE COMPANIES OR REAL ESTATE AGENTS THAT WE KNOW OR HAVE HEARD OF AND DEBATE WHETHER TO CALL THESE FOLKS AND FORK OVER A COMMISSION OR TO SELL ON OUR OWN AND MAKE THAT LONG AWAITED KILLING SO WE CAN BOAST TO OUR NEIGHBORS HOW WE GOT THE HIGHEST PRICE IN THE NEIGHBORHOOD. ACTUALLY, BOTH SCENARIOS ARE PUTTING THE CART AHEAD OF THE HORSE.

WHAT I WOULD DO IS CALL SOME BANKS AND ASK THEM WHO DOES THEIR RESIDENTIAL APPRAISALS. ASK AROUND AND CALL PERHAPS FOUR APPRAISERS AND ASK THEM IF THEY DO F.H.A. APPRAISALS. ASK IF THEY HAVE A DESIGNATION OR A STATE LICENSE, A DESIGNATION, HOWEVER, IS NOT A NECESSITY FOR BEING A GOOD APPRAISER. ASK THE PRICE OF A REGULAR APPRAISAL ACCEPTED BY H.U.D., INTERVIEW THEM EVEN OVER THE PHONE, AND ARRANGE FOR AN APPRAISAL TO BE DONE ON

YOUR HOME OR FOR A 2-PAGE NARRATIVE THAT WILL COST LESS.

THE REASON I SAY THIS IS THAT MANY REAL ESTATE AGENTS DON'T KNOW HOW TO PROPERLY PRICE A HOME. THERE ARE FEW COURSES ON THIS OUTSIDE OF APPRAISAL COURSES, AND MOST AGENTS HAVE TO LEARN THIS AS A SIXTH SENSE OVER TIME. IN ADDITION, MARKETS MAY RISE OR DROP RAPIDLY DUE TO EXTERNAL ECONOMIC FACTORS (LOSS OF A MAJOR EMPLOYER, AS AN EXAMPLE). THERE ARE MANY NEW REALTORS WHO COME AND GO, AND MANY PART TIMERS WHO ARE ROUTINELY INACCURATE. THIS IS ONE OF THE REASONS FOR THE GLUT OF OVERPRICED HOMES SITTING ON THE MARKET ACROSS THE COUNTRY. THEN THERE IS ANOTHER PROBLEM I CALL COMPETITIVE PRICING. WHEN YOU CALL AN AGENT TO GIVE YOU A "FREE MARKET ANALYSIS," HE OR SHE KNOWS FULL WELL THAT YOU HAVE 3 OR 4 OTHER AGENTS COMING OVER LATER, AND THEY WANT TO COME IN AS HIGH AS POSSIBLE. BY THE TIME THE OTHER AGENTS LEAVE, YOUR HOME IS $10,000 OVERPRICED SINCE ALL OF THE AGENTS ARE TRYING TO GET YOUR LISTING AND THE ACCURACY OF REAL VALUE IS

GONE. "I DIDN'T THINK MY HOUSE WAS WORTH THIS MUCH," YOU HAPPILY SAY TO YOUR WIFE. THE AGENTS ARE BANKING ON YOUR GREED, WHICH IS PART OF ALL OF US, AND HOPING YOU'LL GO WITH THEM AND THEIR COMPANY. AFTER YOU SIGN FOR 3 OR 6 MONTHS, THEY WILL THEN TRY TO "WORK ON YOU" TO LOWER THE PRICE BACK TO WHERE IT SHOULD HAVE BEEN IN THE FIRST PLACE AND EFFECT A SALE. THIS IS WHERE YOUR CURRENT APPRAISAL COMES IN TO PLAY.

EVEN IF THE PROFESSIONAL APPRAISAL COSTS YOU $250.00, CHANCES ARE YOU CAN SELL IT TO YOUR BUYER WHO NORMALLY PAYS FOR IT ANYWAY AS LONG AS IT'S NOT MORE THAN SIX MONTHS OLD. IN ADDITION, WHEN OFFERS COME IN, YOU HAVE A CURRENT APPRAISAL TO COUNTER THE BUYER'S CRIES OF HOW LITTLE VALUE YOUR HOUSE REALLY HAS. IF YOU WANT TO HAVE FUN AFTER HAVING THE APPRAISAL DONE, START CALLING REAL ESTATE AGENTS AND SEE IF WHAT I'M SAYING IS CORRECT ABOUT THEIR PRICE SUGGESTION. YOU'LL BE SURPRISED.

NOW THAT YOUR HOME IS PRICED CORRECTLY AND COMPETITIVELY, IT'S TIME TO DECIDE HOW TO

MARKET YOUR PROPERTY. UNLESS YOU ARE AN ATTORNEY, A MORTGAGE LOAN PROCESSOR OR A REAL ESTATE AGENT WITH SOME EXPERIENCE, DON'T FLATTER YOURSELF THINKING YOU CAN SELL YOUR HOME ON YOUR OWN. IF YOU'RE THE TYPE WHO WOULD RATHER TRADE IN YOUR USED CAR THAN SELL IT YOURSELF, DEFINITELY FORGET ABOUT IT.

CONTACT APPROXIMATELY 4 REAL ESTATE COMPANIES FOR INTERVIEWS. LOOK FOR NAMES OF AGENTS YOU SEE DOING BUSINESS IN YOUR AREA. AN AGENT DEALING WITH HOMES IN YOUR AREA IS MORE LIKELY TO PRICE YOUR HOME PROPERLY AND HAVE CUSTOMERS FOR THAT AREA. IT MAKES LITTLE DIFFERENCE WHETHER YOU INTERVIEW LARGE COMPANIES OR SMALL ONES SINCE AGENTS ARE INDEPENDENT CONTRACTORS. AGAIN, CHECK THE EDUCATIONAL BACKGROUND OF THE AGENTS YOU INTERVIEW. ARE THEY A BROKER, G.R.I., C.R.S. OR C.R.B., OR JUST A SALES ASSOCIATE. I HAVE FOUND THAT A PERSON WHO TAKES THE TIME TO OBTAIN A REAL ESTATE EDUCATION GENERALLY IS MORE AGGRESSIVE, HAS MORE ANSWERS, AND CAN STAY WITH A PROPERTY THROUGH CLOSING. ON THE OTHER HAND, YOU MAY WANT TO STAY AWAY FROM

AN AGENT WHO IS TOO BUSY SINCE SOME DO NOT HAVE TIME TO ACTIVELY MARKET AND DO NOT KEEP IN TOUCH WITH CLIENTS. ONE PARTY THAT RELISTED WITH ME TOLD ME THAT THEY INITIALLY LISTED WITH ANOTHER AGENT AT A LARGER COMPANY BECAUSE THE AGENT SEEMED TO BE DOING A LOT OF BUSINESS, WHICH WAS TRUE. THAT AGENT, HOWEVER, AFTER TAKING THE LISTING, NEVER CALLED THE HOMEOWNER FOR 2 MONTHS, AND NEVER RETURNED CALLS EITHER. THIS IS A MAJOR NO-NO, EVEN IF JUST TO TELL A CUSTOMER THAT YOU'RE STILL IN THE COUNTRY. A CALL TO EACH LISTING ONCE A WEEK IS GOOD POLICY FOR AN AGENT.

ASK THE AGENT HOW OFTEN THEY WILL ADVERTISE AND IN WHAT MEDIUMS, AND ASK ABOUT OPEN HOUSES. ALTHOUGH IT (IS TRUE THAT OPEN HOUSES ARE FOR THE BENEFIT OF THE AGENT IN GETTING CUSTOMERS, IF A HOUSE IS PRICED COMPETITIVELY, IT IS VERY POSSIBLE TO SELL A HOME DURING AN OPEN HOUSE.

WHAT IF THE COMPANY SELLS YOUR HOME WITHOUT THE ASSISTANCE OF ANOTHER COMPANY, NO CO-BROKE IN OTHER WORDS. WILL THEY CHARGE

Buyers and Sellers Real Estate Handbook

YOU LESS COMMISSION SINCE THERE IS NO OTHER COMPANY TO SPLIT WITH? IF YOU DO YOUR OWN OPEN HOUSES, WILL THEY CHARGE LESS? THERE IS A GROWING TREND IN REAL ESTATE TODAY CALLED "FEE FOR SERVICE" WHERE YOU ONLY PAY FOR CERTAIN PROVIDED SERVICES "A LA CARTE," INSTEAD OF THE FULL COMMISSION. AS A SELLER, YOU SHOULD MAKE BUYERS AND YOUR AGENT AWARE OF ANY MATERIAL DEFECT ABOUT THE PROPERTY THAT MIGHT AFFECT ITS SALE; HOWEVER, YOU ARE NOT ON TRIAL WITH EVERY BUYER, SO DON'T ACT LIKE YOU'VE JUST SWALLOWED TRUTH SERUM AND TALK ABOUT PROBLEMS WITH THE NEIGHBORS, ETC. SOMETIMES SELLERS ARE THEIR OWN WORST ENEMY IN THAT REGARD. REAL ESTATE AGENTS KNOW WHEN TO SPEAK AND WHEN TO BE QUIET, THE AVERAGE PERSON DOESN'T IN THIS ARENA.

YOU WILL BE ASKED IF A SIGN IN FRONT IS OK AND A LOCK BOX, AS WELL. THE MAJOR OBJECTIONS THAT I ENCOUNTER WITH THESE TWO ITEMS IS THAT A SIGN WOULD TIP THE NEIGHBORS OFF THAT YOU ARE SELLING. FIRST OF ALL, THE NEIGHBORS MAY BE GLAD THAT YOU ARE SELLING AND MAY KNOW

SOMEONE WHO MIGHT BE INTERESTED IN THE AREA. MOREOVER, THEY WILL BE ON THE PHONE TO OTHER NEIGHBORS BEFORE THE REAL ESTATE AGENT LEAVES YOUR HOME – COUNT ON IT. MANY BUYERS ROUTINELY CRUISE A SPECIFIC AREA BECAUSE THEY WANT TO LIVE THERE; A SIGN HELPS IN EVERY WAY. POINT TWO, THE FEAR OF A LOCK BOX IS UNWARRANTED. PUT AWAY YOUR DIAMOND RINGS AND MONEY IF THEY LAY OUT ON A TABLE. IF THEY ARE OUT, YOU ARE ASKING FOR TROUBLE ANYWAY. EVERY CUSTOMER WHO ENTERS VIA A LOCK BOX IS ESCORTED BY A RESPONSIBLE AGENT. THE LIKELIHOOD OF THEM USING YOUR JACUZZI IS REMOTE. A LOCK BOX MAKES YOUR HOME ACCESSIBLE AT ANY HOUR TO HELP WITH A QUICK SALE AT THE HIGHEST PRICE. SO DON'T LIMIT YOURSELF. OBVIOUSLY, IF YOU HAVE A FEROCIOUS DOG, A LOCK BOX IS NOT ADVISABLE UNLESS YOU CAN KEEP THE MUTT OUTSIDE WHILE YOU'RE AT WORK.

IN YOUR INTERVIEW, YOU MIGHT WANT TO ASK A POTENTIAL REAL ESTATE AGENT WHY THEY ENTERED THE BUSINESS IN THE FIRST PLACE. YOU WANT AN AGENT WHO WANTS TO MAKE A GOOD

LIVING MOVING REAL ESTATE. THAT REQUIRES VOLUME OF SALES. MOST REAL ESTATE AGENTS WHO HAVE BEEN IN THE BUSINESS ANY LENGTH OF TIME CAN TELL YOU HOW MISERABLE SOME SELLERS BECOME DURING THE HOME SELLING PROCESS AND HOW SOME BUYERS TURN INTO DR. JEKYLL SOON AFTER THE PURCHASE OFFER IS ACCEPTED. A SUCCESSFUL AGENT'S JOB AS A BUSINESSMAN OR WOMAN IS TO ADVERTISE THE PROPERTY, BRING TWO PARTIES TOGETHER, GET ONE TO THE BANK, NOTIFY THE ATTORNEYS, AND GO ON TO THE NEXT DEAL. IN THE LONG RUN, THE AGENT HAS HELPED BOTH PARTIES, BUT RARELY DO WE GET ANY "PATS ON THE BACK." THE SELLERS WILL ALWAYS TALK ABOUT HOW MUCH MORE MONEY THEY SHOULD HAVE RECEIVED AND HOW MUCH THEY PAID IN COMMISSION; AND THE BUYERS WILL ALWAYS MOAN ABOUT HOW PRESSURED THEY FELT, AND THAT THEY DIDN'T KNOW THIS OR THAT ABOUT THE HOME OR THE NEIGHBORHOOD. SO IF YOU ARE AN AGENT, STOP TRYING TO PLEASE EVERYBODY AND GET OUT THERE AND SELL! AN AGENT MUST ACT LIKE A BUSINESS PERSON AND PUT EMOTIONS ASIDE. DON'T GET INVOLVED IN A BUYER OR SELLERS PERSONAL

PROBLEMS, AND DON'T LET THEM DRAG YOU INTO COMMISSION CUTS AND OTHER GIVE BACKS. PEOPLE WOULD NEVER ASK THEIR DOCTOR OR LAWYER TO TAKE A CUT IN FEES OR COMMISSION, YET THINK NOTHING OF ASKING THAT OF THEIR REAL ESTATE AGENT. IF YOU GET TO CLOSE TO THEM, YOU'LL HAVE A HARD TIME SAYING NO.

THE BENEFIT I HAVE FOUND OF LISTING WITH A LARGER COMPANY IS THAT THEY CAN AFFORD MORE ADVERTISING. MORE NEIGHBORHOOD MAILOUTS, MORE T.V. ADVERTISING AND CAN, IN SHORT, MORE THOROUGHLY SATURATE THE MARKET TO QUICKEN YOUR SALE AT THE HIGHEST POSSIBLE PRICE.

ONCE YOUR PROPERTY IS ON THE MARKET, GIVE YOURSELF A COUPLE OF WEEKS AND MONITOR THE ACTIVITY. HAVE THERE BEEN MANY PEOPLE THROUGH THE HOME? IF NOT, DON'T WORRY, GIVE YOURSELF ANOTHER 2 WEEKS BEFORE CONSIDERING A PRICE ADJUSTMENT. PROVIDING YOU HAVE OVERCOME THE GREED FACTOR AND PUT YOUR HOME ON THE MARKET COMPETITIVELY PRICED, YOU MAY WANT TO ADJUST THE PRICE (ALWAYS DOWNWARD) 5- 10% EVERY MONTH UNTIL IT SELLS. IF YOUR HOUSE IS WORTH ITS INITIAL PRICE, IT WILL

SELL IN 60 DAYS. IF I TAKE A LISTING THAT IS OVERPRICED, I TELL THE OWNER UP FRONT THAT I WILL ONLY ADVERTISE IT ONCE IN THE NEWSPAPER AND DO NO OPEN HOUSES UNTIL WE SEE WHAT KIND OF ACTIVITY WE GET ON THE PROPERTY. ONCE THE OWNER SEES FOR HIMSELF THAT NO ONE IS COMING THROUGH HIS CASTLE, HE THEN SOMETIMES COMES BACK DOWN TO REALITY AND LOWERS THE PRICE. I REFUSE TO THROW MY MONEY DOWN THE DRAIN ON AN OVERPRICED LISTING. AND I REFUSE TO DEPRIVE MY KIDS OF THEIR DADDY ON SUNDAY AFTERNOON TO SIT IN AN OVERPRICED LISTING READING GOOD HOUSEKEEPING. HOWEVER, I TELL THE OWNER UP FRONT THAT THIS IS THE CASE.

AS A SELLER YOU CAN OFFER TO PAY POINTS FOR THE BUYER OR PART OF CLOSING COSTS; HOWEVER, ON F.H.A. OR V.A. LOANS, THE SELLER IS LIMITED ON HOW MUCH OF THESE COSTS HE CAN PAY. YOU CAN OFFER THE SELLING AGENT AN AIRPLANE TICKET, A LAWN MOWER, OR A CASH BONUS, ANYTHING YOU WANT TO, AS AN INCENTIVE TO SELL YOUR PROPERTY. IF YOU DO THIS, MAKE SURE YOU ARE COMMITTED TO THE EXTRAS ONLY IF YOU GET YOUR PRICE.

Alan Ray Hoxie

I WAS TALKING TO A FRIEND WHO HAD A HOME FOR SALE OUTSIDE OF BUFFALO. HE HAD BEEN TRANSFERRED. IT HAD BEEN ON THE MARKET FOR 1-2 YEARS WITH LITTLE ACTIVITY. I TOLD HIM TO OFFER A BONUS OF $500 TO THE SELLING AGENT FOR AN ACCEPTABLE OFFER. HE CALLED HIS AGENT AND THEY MADE THE CHANGE IN THE LOCAL M.L.S. LISTING. HE HAD TWO OFFERS THE NEXT WEEK; ONE, HE ACCEPTED.

FOR SALE BY OWNER

ONE OF THE MOST COMMON REASONS PEOPLE TRY TO SELL THEIR HOMES ON THEIR OWN, IS OBVIOUSLY THE COMMISSION. THIS IS A REAL CONCERN, AND I CAN'T KNOCK IT EXCEPT TO TRY TO EXPLAIN LOGICALLY WHY THE COMMISSION PAID IS REALLY WORTH IT. REAL ESTATE AGENTS HAVE MANY PRE-QUALIFIED CUSTOMERS THAT THEY WORK WITH AND SUBSCRIBE, GENERALLY, TO A M.L.S. SERVICE. I DON'T EVEN BEGIN TO SHOW HOMES TO A CUSTOMER UNTIL THEY ARE QUALIFIED BY A BANKER AND THEIR CREDIT IS CHECKED. THIS WAY, WHEN WE GO IN WITH AN OFFER, THE SELLER AND LISTING AGENT ARE MUCH MORE COMFORTABLE IN KNOWING THAT WE'VE DONE OUR HOMEWORK, AND WE KNOW THAT WE'RE NOT SPINNING OUR WHEELS. EACH YEAR I INITIALLY GET A HALF DOZEN CUSTOMERS WHO PROCLAIM THAT THEIR CREDIT IS GOOD ONLY TO HAVE THEIR REPORT DELIVERED IN A WHEELBARROW. COVER YOUR BASES, UP FRONT.

IN SHORT, AGENTS ARE WORKING WITH REAL QUALIFIED BUYERS, NOT TIRE KICKERS. AS A SELLER ON YOUR OWN YOU DON'T KNOW WHO YOU'RE

LETTING IN THE DOOR. IT COULD BE SOMEONE CASING YOUR HOME FOR A LATER BURGLARY OR WORSE. IF YOU FIND A BUYER, WHO WILL QUALIFY THE PERSON? IF YOU INSIST ON SELLING YOUR OWN HOME, YOU CAN CALL ANY BANK OR MORTGAGE BROKER AND THEY WOULD BE HAPPY TO SIT IN YOUR HOME TO QUALIFY ANY PROSPECTS DURING AN OPEN HOUSE, THEY WILL NOT, HOWEVER, DRAW UP THE CONTRACT UNLESS THEY HAVE A VALID REAL ESTATE LICENSE. THIS YOUR LAWYER CAN DO AFTER THE INTERESTED PARTY QUALIFIES FINANCIALLY.

WHAT IF THEY HAVE A HOME TO SELL? WHAT THEN? DO YOU KEEP IN TOUCH WITH THEIR AGENT IF YOU ACCEPT THE OFFER WITH A CONTINGENCY? (SEE CHAPTER 11 ON WHAT IS A CONTINGENCY) THE JOB STARTS FOR ANY REAL ESTATE AGENT AFTER THE CONTRACT IS SIGNED BY BOTH PARTIES. THE REAL WORK IS MAKING SURE THE BUYERS SUBMIT ALL REQUESTED PAPERWORK TO THE BANK. IF THERE NEEDS TO BE CO-SIGNERS, WHAT ABOUT THAT? WITH BANKS TIGHTENING THEIR QUALIFICATIONS, THERE IS A LOT OF WORK AN AGENT HAS TO DO TO SEE A DEAL THROUGH TO CLOSING, INCLUDING KEEPING IN TOUCH WITH THE LAWYERS FROM THE BANK AND

FROM BOTH PARTIES. REAL ESTATE DEALS, I FEEL, ARE NOT TOP PRIORITY FOR ATTORNEYS SINCE WHAT THEY MAKE ON THEM IS MINIMAL AND, IF THEY ARE NOT CONTACTED REGULARLY, THESE THINGS MAY FALL ON THE BACK BURNER.

GENERALLY, THE BEST REASON TO USE A REALTOR IN THE SALE OF YOUR HOME IS FOR THE PROFESSIONAL, SATURATED MARKETING AVAILABLE. THE M.L.S. SYSTEM IS A 24-HOUR WAREHOUSE OF INFORMATION ABOUT MANY HOMES AVAILABLE TO ANY MEMBER AGENT AT ANY TIME. ANY PROFESSIONAL COMPANY BELONGS TO AN M.L.S. SYSTEM IN THEIR AREA.

I SOLD A HOUSE FOR THE PARENTS OF ONE OF MY LONG TIME FRIENDS. I HEARD THAT HE WAS SELLING BY OWNER, SO I DROVE OVER TO SEE HIM. HE WAS SITTING IN A LAWN CHAIR INSIDE HIS GARAGE, HAVING A GARAGE SALE WITH A FOR SALE SIGN IN HIS FRONT YARD. I ASKED HIM WHAT HE WAS DOING, AND HE TOLD ME THAT HE HOPED THAT SOMEONE GOING TO HIS FREQUENT GARAGE SALES WOULD ALSO BE LOOKING FOR A HOUSE. FAT CHANCE, I CAN HEAR IT NOW. "WELL MISTER, I WAS REALLY IN THE MARKET FOR A LAWN MOWER, BUT WHILE I'M AT IT,

Alan Ray Hoxie

I'LL TAKE THAT HOUSE, TOO." HE IS NOT AN IGNORANT MAN ORDINARILY, BUT I COULDN'T BELIEVE MY EARS. I LISTED THE HOME AND WE HAD TO REDUCE THE PRICE TWICE BY A TOTAL OF $8,000 AND IT FINALLY SOLD 4 MONTHS LATER.

WHILE READING THIS MORNINGS PAPER, THERE WAS AN ARTICLE ON HOW BAD THE REAL ESTATE MARKET IS IN THE NORTHEAST. A COUPLE HAD THEIR HOME ON THE MARKET FOR $229,000 FOR A WHILE AND REDUCED IT TO $199,000. THEIR COMMENT TO THE REPORTER WAS THAT THEY WILL WAIT UNTIL THE MARKET GETS BETTER. THEY SPOKE ABOUT THE MARKET AS IF IT WAS SOMETHING FOREIGN OR IN OUTER SPACE. IN THEIR CASE, THIS WAS TRUE SINCE THE PRICE OF THEIR HOME WAS STILL FAR ABOVE THE COMPARABLE SALES OF THEIR AREA. THEY INTENTIONALLY PUT THEMSELVES OUT OF THE MARKET. MAYBE, SUBCONSCIOUSLY, THEY REALLY DIDN'T WANT TO SELL. BUT THAT SEEMS TOO OBVIOUS. I KNOW THE AREA WHERE THEIR HOME IS AND ANYONE WITH $199,000 SURE AS HECK WOULDN'T BUY THERE. THEY COULD BUILD NEW AND ALMOST EQUAL IN SQUARE FOOTAGE IN MOST OTHER AREAS IN OUR COUNTY.

HOWEVER, THEY SAY, WE'RE IN NO HURRY SO WE CAN WAIT. ANOTHER MISTAKE IS TO THINK THAT YOU CAN WAIT ANY LENGTH OF TIME AND THAT IT WON'T HURT YOUR CHANCES OF AN EVENTUAL SALE. THE LONGER YOUR HOME SITS, THE MORE "STALE" IT BECOMES. THE LONGER IT SITS, THE MORE INTENTLY PROSPECTIVE BUYERS WILL WONDER "WHAT'S WRONG WITH THIS HOUSE THAT OTHERS HAVE SEEN" AND SAY, "I WONDER IF I'M MAKING A MISTAKE." THERE IS A DIRECT RELATIONSHIP BETWEEN HOW LONG A HOUSE SITS AND HOW MANY BUYERS ARE FRIGHTENED AWAY BECAUSE OF THEIR OWN UNCERTAINTY AND INSECURITY, EVEN WHEN THE PRICE IS OF NO OBJECTION. I FIND MANY HOMES TODAY ARE OVERPRICED BECAUSE THE HOME EQUITY LOAN, COMBINED WITH THE FIRST MORTGAGE, DOESN'T EVEN LEAVE THE SELLER ROOM TO PAY A COMMISSION. MANY COMMISSIONS TODAY ARE PAID OUT OF POCKET. SOME NOT AT ALL.

HOWEVER, BUYERS ARE NOT RESPONSIBLE FOR A SELLERS FINANCIAL WOES AND WON'T MAKE AN OFFER ON AN OVERPRICED HOME.

AN EXPERIENCED REALTOR WILL ALSO GO THROUGH YOUR HOME AND POINT OUT AREAS THAT

NEED ATTENTION OR CORRECTION BEFORE IT IS PUT ON THE MARKET. THOSE CRACKS AND HOLES THAT YOU'VE IGNORED FOR YEARS WOULD BE POINTED OUT BY A REALTOR SO THAT YOUR HOME IS OPTIMALLY MARKETABLE. THAT DIRTY GOLD SHAG RUG IN THE HALLWAY, FOR EXAMPLE, MAY BE HIDING A RATHER BEAUTIFUL HARDWOOD FLOOR THAT IS IN GOOD SHAPE.

BUYERS HAVE A GREAT DEAL OF KNOWLEDGE ABOUT WHAT PROPERTY IS WORTH IN THEIR AREA OF INTEREST SINCE THEY ARE ACTIVELY AND INTENSELY IN THE MIX FOR A PERIOD OF TIME. ALL BUYERS RECOGNIZE AN OVERPRICED HOME SINCE IT STICKS OUT LIKE A SORE THUMB. REALTORS CAN AND WILL REGULARLY ADVISE THE SELLER ON PRICE ADJUSTMENTS BASED ON WHAT THE AGENT SEES SELLING IN THAT AREA OF A COMPARABLE NATURE.

ANOTHER OPTION IS TO CONTACT REAL ESTATE COMPANIES IN YOUR AREA AND OFFER TO PAY ½ THE NORMAL COMMISSION TO A SELLING COMPANY. THIS COULD SAVE SOME EXPENSE IN COMMISSION, BUT WHEN YOU ADD IN YOUR ADVERTISING COSTS, YOUR TIME ANSWERING INQUIRY ONLY PHONE CALLS, AND HOLDING OPEN HOUSES, YOU WON'T HAVE SAVED

THAT MUCH. AS FOR PRICING YOUR HOME 5% BELOW MARKET AND TAKING THE HIGHEST BID, BUYERS KNOW THE MARKET AND WILL NOT PAY MORE FOR YOUR HOME THAN OTHERS IN THE NEIGHBORHOOD AND WANT A BARGAIN TO BOOT. THE ONLY WAY TO MOVE IT FAST IS AT A GOOD PRICE FOR ANY BUYER. THIS WAY YOU WILL PROBABLY GET MULTIPLE OFFERS IN THE HANDS OF REAL ESTATE AND THEY MAY EVEN BE ABOVE ASKING PRICE. WITH LITTLE EXPENSE OR TIME SPENT ON YOUR PART, BEST LEFT TO THE PROFESSIONALS. PRICE IT A TAD LOW, WATCH IT GO

Alan Ray Hoxie

NOTHING DOWN, NOTHING DOING

EVERY TIME WE TURN ON OUR T.V., ESPECIALLY ON SATURDAY OR SUNDAY MORNING, WE SEE THE SMILING FACE OF ED OR DAVE OR CARLTON, INTRODUCING US TO A PANEL OF ORDINARY FOLKS JUST LIKE YOU AND ME WHO CLAIM TO HAVE MADE THOUSANDS OF DOLLARS IN REAL ESTATE. THEY HAVE QUIT THEIR DAY JOBS TO LOLL IN THE SUN IN HAWAII AND COUNT THEIR MONEY WHILE BOASTING OF THEIR VAST PORTFOLIOS.

DOES IT SOUND TOO GOOD TO BE TRUE? WELL, AS THE SAYING GOES, IF IT SOUNDS TOO GOOD TO BE TRUE, IT PROBABLY IS. NOT THAT THESE GENTLEMEN ARE NOT TELLING THE TRUTH REGARDING WAYS TO ACQUIRE REAL ESTATE AND NOT THAT THE PANEL ARE LIARS. IT IS SIMPLY THAT EVEN A BLIND SQUIRREL GETS AN ACORN NOW AND THEN, AND THESE PEOPLE ARE TELLING YOU ONLY ONE SIDE OF THE STORY.

IN MY INTRODUCTION, I EXPLAINED THAT WE ARE A NATION OF COUCH POTATOES AND BUTTON PUSHERS, ARMED WITH DEADLY CREDIT CARDS WHO BY MERELY DIALING AN 800 NUMBER AND FORKING

OVER $300 - $400 FOR TAPES AND BOOKS, CAN BECOME THE NEXT TRUMP OF OUR NEIGHBORHOOD. THESE PEOPLE ON T.V. KNOW HOW LAZY WE ARE AS CONSUMERS AND KNOW ALSO THAT, MOTIVATED BY OUR GREED AND OUR DESIRE TO GET RICH QUICK, THEY CAN BLAST INTO OUR CREDIT CARD ACCOUNTS AND COME OUT SMELLING LIKE A ROSE. I AM A REAL ESTATE BROKER, COLLEGE GRADUATE, HAVE A G.R.I. DESIGNATION AND DO APPRAISALS AND STILL I AM OVERWHELMED AT THE VOLUME OF WHAT IS SENT IN THOSE PACKAGES OF TAPES AND FORMS. THE AVERAGE PERSON WHO BUYS THOSE TAPES WILL FIND THEM COLLECTING DUST IN A CORNER FOR MANY YEARS. WHY? BECAUSE WE BARELY HAVE TIME TO MANAGE OUR HOME AND WORK LIVES, LET ALONE TO GO OUT AND PREVIEW FORECLOSURE PROPERTY AND NO MONEY DOWN DEALS. WHY DON'T THESE T.V. GENIUSES HAVE THEIR PANEL SIT IN A LOBBY OF A DEAL GONE BAD OR THE LOBBY OF AN APARTMENT BUILDING FULL OF ANGRY TENANTS. I HAVE OWNED PROPERTY FOR TEN YEARS, AND IT TOOK ME FIVE YEARS TO BECOME COMFORTABLE WITH IT AND NOT LET IT GET ME DOWN. I WILL GIVE YOU TWO SCENARIOS POPULAR WITH THE T.V.

SHOWS AND EXPLAIN WHY THESE ARE VERY DIFFICULT TO FIND, LET ALONE TO PROFIT FROM. KEEP IN MIND THAT THE EXAMPLES YOU HEAR ON T.V. ARE A VERY SMALL PERCENTAGE OF REAL SITUATIONS. KEEP IN MIND ALSO THAT IF REAL ESTATE DEALS WERE SUCH A GOOD DEAL AS IS BELIEVED, THE SAVINGS & LOANS IN THIS COUNTRY WOULDN'T BE IN SUCH BAD SHAPE SINCE MOST OF THEM LOST ON REAL ESTATE DEALS. FIRST OF ALL, LET'S TALK ABOUT FORECLOSURES.

MOST FORECLOSURES ARE OVERPRICED. THIS IS IN PART DUE TO UNREALISTIC APPRAISALS RESULTING IN TOO HIGH A MORTGAGE BEING GIVEN IN THE FIRST PLACE, AND THE PROPERTY THEN IS "MILKED OUT" BY AN INVESTOR. SOMEONE PRIOR TO FORECLOSURE HAS TAKEN THE MONEY AND WALKED. I GET THE H.U.D. FORECLOSURE LIST EACH WEEK FOR MY COUNTY. THERE IS NOT ONE FORECLOSURE I HAVE SEEN THAT IS PRICED WELL BELOW MARKET VALUE FOR THE AREA. IN ADDITION, FOR INVESTORS MANY OF THESE ARE "CASH ONLY" DEALS. THEY ARE NOT ELIGIBLE FOR F.H.A. LOANS. MANY OF THESE ARE IN MARGINAL NEIGHBORHOODS AND HAVE MANY CODE VIOLATIONS. IN CASES

WHERE THERE IS F.H.A. FINANCING, YOU WOULD STILL HAVE TO BE QUALIFIED AS A REGULAR PURCHASER WOULD, SO WHERE IS THE DEAL? HOW DID THE APPRAISAL GET OUT OF WHACK TO BEGIN WITH? THE LONG AND SHORT OF THIS IS THAT APPRAISERS DON'T WANT TO BLOW DEALS MADE BY REAL ESTATE AGENTS, AND BANKS WANT TO DO BUSINESS FOR THE IMMEDIATE PROFIT CONTAINED IN CLOSING COSTS. COMBINE THAT THEN WITH A DECLINING MARKET SINCE 1989, EVERYTHING CLICKS AND EVERYBODY IS HAPPY UNTIL THE NEW OWNER DECIDES THAT EITHER HE CAN'T COLLECT THE RENT BECAUSE THE TENANTS WON'T PAY, OR REPAIRS BECOME TOO COSTLY OR THE HOME HAS MANY CODE VIOLATIONS THAT MUST BE REPAIRED. THE OWNER WALKS AWAY FROM THE HOUSE AND FORECLOSURE BEGINS. H.U.D. IS STUCK WITH A HIGH MORTGAGE AT OR ABOVE MARKET FOR THE AREA. THIS IS A SMALL BUT SIMILAR EXAMPLE OF THE WHOLE SAVINGS AND LOAN CRISIS. BANKS LENT TOO MUCH MONEY ON THE CURRENT VALUE OF THE PROPERTY; AND IT WAS NOT, AT THE TIME, WORTH IT OR DID NOT APPRECIATE FAST ENOUGH TO COVER THE DEBT, LARGELY BASED ON FAULTY APPRAISALS OR ON

NONE AT ALL AND THE ANTICIPATION OF A STEADY GROWTH MARKET.

NEXT, LET'S LOOK AT "NO MONEY DOWN DEALS." DID YOU EVER HEAR, "IF IT SOUNDS TOO GOOD TO BE TRUE, IT PROBABLY IS." WE CAN MODIFY THAT A LITTLE AND SAY THAT IF YOU BUY A PROPERTY FOR NOTHING DOWN, THAT'S PROBABLY WHAT IT'S WORTH. I HAVE A FEW TWO FAMILY HOMES CURRENTLY WHERE MY CASH FLOW IS ONLY $300 A MONTH PROFIT. HOWEVER, THE TENANTS ARE GOOD; I HAVE NO PROBLEMS WITH THE HOUSES. I REALIZE THE PROPERTY AS LONG TERM INVESTMENTS. FOR ME TO SELL THEM "NO MONEY DOWN" WOULDN'T MAKE SENSE, ESPECIALLY FROM A TAX STANDPOINT. THESE PROPERTIES ARE MORE VALUABLE IN REDUCING MY TAX LIABILITY AT YEAR END THAN THE MONEY I STICK IN MY POCKET. NO INVESTOR OR ATTORNEY FOR AN INVESTOR WOULD ALLOW A PROPERTY TO BE TRANSFERRED FOR NOTHING DOWN. PRIMARILY, ONLY PROPERTIES THAT HAVE NO BANK MORTGAGE WOULD BE SOLD NO MONEY DOWN SINCE BANKS GENERALLY HAVE A "DUE ON SALE" CLAUSE UPON TRANSFER OF THE PROPERTY. THE ONLY REASON YOU MAY BE ABLE TO FIND A

PROPERTY OF THIS TYPE IS THAT THE CURRENT OWNER HAS BECOME A "DON'T WANTER," AS REAL ESTATE AUTHOR BOB ALLEN CALLS THEM. THE AMAZING THING TO ME IS HOW ORDINARY CITIZENS WITH NO BACKGROUND IN REAL ESTATE AND NO EXPERIENCE OWNING AND MANAGING PROPERTY THINK THAT THEY WILL BE ANY LESS OF A "DON'T WANTER" THAN THE PERSON LOOKING TO GET OUT FROM UNDER THAT PROPERTY IN THE FIRST PLACE. IF A PROPERTY IS UP TO PAR AND THERE ARE GOOD TENANTS AND THERE IS A POSITIVE CASH FLOW, YOU WILL NEVER GET IT FOR NOTHING DOWN, YOU CAN COUNT ON IT. AND IF IT IS IN THE HANDS OF A REAL ESTATE COMPANY, YOU WILL AT LEAST HAVE TO PAY THE COMMISSION.

WHAT YOU WILL GET WHEN YOU LOOK FOR ZERO DOWN PROPERTY IS A PROPERTY SOMEONE IS TRYING DESPERATELY TO RUN AWAY FROM. YOU WILL HAVE A PROPERTY WITH TENANTS WHO DON'T PAY RENT AND WHO DESTROY OR HAVE DESTROYED THE PROPERTY. YOU WILL HAVE A HOUSE THAT IS IN VIOLATION OF LOCAL CODES, A SITUATION WHOSE REMEDY NOW BELONGS TO THE NEW OWNER. HERE IS AN EXAMPLE THAT HAPPENED TO ME. MY FATHER

AND I ASSUMED AN F.H.A. MORTGAGE FOR $2,000. THE OWNER, AT MY REQUEST, HAD REFINANCED THE OWNER OCCUPIED 2 FAMILY SINCE HE ONLY OWED A FEW THOUSAND DOLLARS ON IT, HE GOT HIS MONEY AND WE GOT IN FOR ONLY $2,000. I THOUGHT WE HAD PULLED A MAJOR COUP, JUST LIKE IN THE REAL ESTATE BOOKS AND TAPES ON T.V. THEN REALITY SET !N. ONE TENANT GOT A LITTLE TICKED OFF AND CALLED THE CITY CODES DEPARTMENT REQUESTING AN INSPECTION, WHICH THEY CAN DO AND, AS A LANDLORD, YOU CANNOT REFUSE AN INSPECTION. THE CITY CAME DOWN AND CITED THE PROPERTY FOR ELECTRICAL DEFICIENCIES. THAT COST US $1,800.00, PLUS WE HAD TO HAVE IT DONE IN 30 DAYS OR THEY WOULD DECLARE IT UNSAFE FOR OCCUPANCY. IN THE MEANTIME, THE UPSTAIRS TENANT WAS ON PUBLIC ASSISTANCE, AND THEY STOPPED RENT PAYMENTS TO US UNTIL THE VIOLATIONS WERE CORRECTED. THESE ARE THINGS YOU DON'T HEAR ABOUT ON T.V. AND ARE MORE THE RULE THAN THE EXCEPTION IN RENTAL PROPERTY OF THIS TYPE. I HAVE SINCE HAD TO WALK AWAY FROM THIS PROPERTY BECAUSE OF DAMAGE AND THE FAILING NEIGHBORHOOD. IT WILL SOON FORECLOSE.

ONE POPULAR SCENARIO ON T.V. IS WHEN A YOUNG MAN STANDS UP, TAKES THE MICROPHONE AND EXPLAINS HOW HE BORROWED $25,000 FROM HIS AUNT, BOUGHT A HOME, REFINANCED IT FOR $50,000.00, PAID HER BACK, AND PUT $25,000 IN HIS POCKET. THE CROWD APPLAUDS, HE SMILES AND SITS DOWN AND THE REAL ESTATE WIZARD RUNNING THE SHOW SAYS, "HOW ABOUT THAT. IF HE CAN DO IT, SO CAN YOU. " BUT THAT STORY IS NOT OVER AS IT APPEARS TO BE SO HAPPILY ON TELEVISION. NOW THIS YOUNG MAN HAS A $50,000 MORTGAGE. IF HE KEEPS THE PROPERTY AND RENTS IT OUT, THE RENTS FOR THAT AREA HAD BETTER COVER THE MORTGAGE, TAXES AND INSURANCE. IF HE LIVES IN IT, HIS NEW MORTGAGE PAYMENTS AT $50,000 HAVE DOUBLED, HE REALLY BORROWED THE MONEY JUST LIKE A LOAN. THERE ARE NO INCOME TAXES ON IT NOW, BUT WHEN HE GOES TO SELL IT, PART OF HIS PROCEEDS MAY BE TAXABLE - IF THERE ARE PROCEEDS. AND WHERE IS THE PROPERTY NOW IN TERMS OF THE SURROUNDING MARKET? IT IS NOW SO HIGHLY FINANCED THAT IT COULD TAKE YEARS TO SELL?

THIS IS WHAT THEY DON'T TELL YOU IN THOSE REAL ESTATE MAIL ORDER COURSES. WHY? BECAUSE THE REALITY IS NOT AS HAPPY A SCENARIO AS STICKING $15,000 RIGHT IN YOUR POCKET. I WILL HAVE TO HOLD ON TO PROPERTY I OWN FOR MANY YEARS UNTIL THE MORTGAGES ARE SUBSTANTIALLY PAID DOWN. THIS IS ALSO WHAT CAUSES MANY LANDLORDS TO WALK AWAY FROM THE PROPERTY. THEY MAY BE HAVING PROBLEMS COLLECTING RENT OR WITH THE LOCAL BUILDING INSPECTOR AND SAY "THE HELL WITH THIS. I GOT AS MUCH AS I COULD OUT OF THE PLACE AND I DON'T WANT TO HOLD ON ANY MORE. " THIS FELLOW IS A PERFECT CANDIDATE FOR YOUR LOW OR NO MONEY DOWN PITCH. BUT REMEMBER, YOU MAY BE ASSUMING A HIGHLY LEVERAGED PROPERTY, AND YOU'VE GOT TO LOOK AT THE POTENTIAL FOR INCREASED RENT FOR A DECENT CASH FLOW AND THE QUALITY OF TENANT THE AREA ATTRACTS.

IF YOU KEEP IN MIND THAT PROPERTY INVESTING SHOULD BE TREATED AS A LONG TERM INVESTMENT, YOU'LL BE FURTHER AHEAD AND LESS DISAPPOINTED. IF YOU HAPPEN TO BUY LOW AND FLIP A PROPERTY FOR A NICE GAIN, GREAT! . BUT IF

YOU DON'T OR CAN'T BECAUSE OF A VARIETY OF FACTORS, YOU HAD BETTER BE WILLING TO "STAY IN THE RING" WITH THE TENANTS, THE CITY, THE BANK, THE NEIGHBORS, ETC. MOST AMERICANS JUST HATE TO HAVE ANYONE MAD AT THEM. IF THAT'S YOU, BUY BONDS AND C.D.,S, NOT REAL ESTATE.

AS I WRITE THIS, HOWEVER, "NOTHING DOWN" OR LITTLE DOWN DEALS WILL INCREASE IN NUMBERS AND I'M NOT SAYING TO STAY AWAY FROM THEM, JUST DO YOU HOMEWORK AND ASK A LOT OF QUESTIONS. WHY WILL THERE BE MORE OF THESE DEALS FLOATING AROUND AND WHY ASK MORE QUESTIONS? FIRST OF ALL, DUE TO THE S&L CRISIS, MANY BANKS AND MORTGAGE LENDERS HAVE TOTALLY DROPPED OUT OF THE LENDING PICTURE ALTOGETHER FOR COMMERCIAL AND NONOWNER OCCUPIED PROPERTIES, PREFERRING INSTEAD TO TAKE THE SAFER ROUTE OF LENDING TO RESIDENTIAL OWNER OCCUPANTS ONLY. EVEN THESE INSTITUTIONS HAVE TIGHTENED THEIR GRIP ON QUALIFICATIONS AND CREDIT CHECKS, AND ARE DEMANDING MORE MONEY DOWN. BECAUSE OF THIS, MANY OWNERS (SELLERS) WILL HAVE NO CHOICE BUT TO HOLD MORTGAGES WITH INCREASING

REGULARITY. THERE WILL BE A GREATER POOL OF "DON'T WANTERS" AND PRIVATE FINANCING WILL BOOM. WHY ASK QUESTIONS? AS I MENTIONED BEFORE, ONCE YOU SIGN THAT CONTRACT TO PURCHASE, YOUR QUESTION ASKING PERIOD SHOULD BE OVER. AS A MATTER OF GOOD NEGOTIATING PRINCIPLE AND TO GIVE YOURSELF ENOUGH TIME TO EXPLORE THE SITUATION, CONVINCE YOURSELF THAT IT MAKES NO DIFFERENCE WHETHER YOU ACQUIRE THAT PROPERTY OR NOT. THIS WILL QUELL YOUR EMOTIONS ABOUT A PIECE OF PROPERTY AND CLEAR YOUR MIND TO ASK IMPORTANT QUESTIONS. A WISE REAL ESTATE TEACHER I ONCE KNEW USED TO SAY, "NEVER FALL IN LOVE WITH INANIMATE OBJECTS", I.E., HOUSES, CARS, ETC., AND "YOU CAN'T MARRY EVERY GIRL YOU DANCE WITH."

IN NEGOTIATING WITH THE SELLER, IT IS VITALLY IMPORTANT NOT ONLY TO ASK QUESTIONS ABOUT THE PROPERTY (I.E., BACK TAXES, CODE VIOLATIONS, MECHANICS LIENS, WATER IN BASEMENT), BUT ALSO TO ASK THE SELLER ABOUT HIMSELF AND SOME OF HIS BACKGROUND AND WHY HE WANTS TO SELL. IF A MAN SAYS HE HAS LOTS OF OTHER PROPERTY BUT HE JUST WANTS TO SELL THIS ONE PIECE, YOU CAN BE

SURE THAT ONE PIECE IS HIS BIGGEST HEADACHE - TRY NOT TO MAKE IT YOURS. ON THE OTHER HAND, A PROPERTY THAT IS OWNER OCCUPIED AND HAS BEEN FOR YEARS IS PROBABLY A SOLID FIND, BUT STILL QUESTIONS SHOULD BE ASKED.

THE LESS YOU ARE PERMITTED TO PUT DOWN ON A PROPERTY, THE MORE APPREHENSIVE YOU SHOULD BE, THE MORE CAREFUL YOU SHOULD BE. ANY GOOD LAWYER WOULD ADVISE HIS CLIENT NOT TO LET A PROPERTY GO FOR UNDER 10% DOWN OF ITS MARKET VALUE OR SALE PRICE. THIS IS BECAUSE THE COST OF FORECLOSURE AND POTENTIAL DAMAGE TO THE PROPERTY ONCE TRANSFERRED COULD BE SUBSTANTIAL. IF A PERSON HAS SOME OF THEIR OWN MONEY INVESTED IN A PROPERTY, THEY ARE LESS LIKELY TO WALK AWAY FROM IT AND/OR DAMAGE THE PROPERTY.

I KNOW MANY INVESTORS WHO TAKE OVER NO MONEY DOWN PROPERTIES AND COLLECT THE RENT FOR A YEAR, DON'T PAY THE TAXES OR WATER, AND HAVE NO INTENTION OF STAYING WITH THE PROPERTY. AFTER THE YEAR, THEY WALK, LEAVING THE (OWNER) MORTGAGE HOLDER WITH A BIG BACK TAX BILL, DAMAGES, ETC.

Alan Ray Hoxie

I PERSONALLY AM IN A SITUATION NOW WHERE 2 YEARS AGO I BOUGHT A 3 FAMILY FROM A FELLOW WHO HAD OWNED IT FOR 20 YEARS. I GAVE HIM $2000 DOWN AND HE AGREED TO A 2 YEAR BALLOON MORTGAGE AMORTIZED OVER 30 YEARS. I HAVE BEEN PAYING HIM MONTHLY AND CLEARING $350 A MONTH ON THIS PROPERTY. HOWEVER, I HAVE NOT PAID THE PROPERTY TAXES ON IT AND OWE THE CITY ABOUT $3,500. NOW I COULD WALK AWAY, FOR EXAMPLE, AND LEAVE HIM WITH THE HOUSE AND A BIG TAX BILL, WHICH HE WOULD PROBABLY TRY TO RECOVER FROM ME. BUT I AM IN THE PROCESS OF PUTTING A BANK MORTGAGE ON THE PROPERTY AND INCLUDE THE CLOSING COSTS AND BACK TAXES IN THE MORTGAGE WHICH THE BANK SAYS I CAN DO. A BANK THAT WILL DO THIS TYPE OF FINANCING IS PROBABLY A SMALL BANK.

MOST SMALL BANKS KEEP THEIR OWN MORTGAGE LOANS AND HAVE MORE FLEXIBLE RULES REGARDING INVESTOR PROPERTIES. RESEARCH LOCAL BANKS TO FIND THE MOST LENIENT - A PHONE CALL WILL DO. YOU WILL PAY A HIGHER INTEREST RATE FOR THEIR RISK, BUT MOST OF THAT YOU WRITE OFF ANYWAY. JUST MAKE SURE

YOU HAVE AT LEAST A $100 PER MONTH CASH FLOW PER RESIDENTIAL UNIT TO COVER OTHER EXPENSES.

THERE ARE OTHER WAYS TO ACQUIRE PROPERTY AND THEN TAKE ADVANTAGE OF THAT LEVERAGE. ONE MOST COMMON FOR THE BEGINNING INVESTOR IS TO OBTAIN A HOME EQUITY LOAN ON YOUR PRESENT HOME, BUY A PROPERTY THAT NEEDS REHABILITATION, FIX IT UP, AND SELL IT TO PAY OFF YOUR HOME EQUITY LOAN AND POCKET THE REST.

IF YOU DECIDE TO KEEP THE PROPERTY AND RENT IT OUT, SIMPLY PUT A MORTGAGE ON IT WHEN YOU'RE DONE WITH THE RENOVATIONS ENOUGH TO COVER YOUR PURCHASE LOAN AND WHATEVER BALANCE REMAINS IN YOUR POCKET OR TOWARDS REPAYMENT OF YOUR HOME EQUITY LOAN. YOU WILL, OF COURSE, MAKE SURE THAT THE RENTAL RECEIVED COVERS THE MORTGAGE, TAXES, INSURANCE AND PUTS A LITTLE IN YOUR POCKET EVERY MONTH. THE TAX CONSEQUENCES OF THIS SECOND APPROACH ARE PREFERABLE, BUT YOU HAVE THE HEADACHE OF TENANT RESPONSIBILITIES.

ANOTHER POPULAR WAY OF ACQUIRING PROPERTY, AND THIS IS IN EVERY "HOW TO GET RICH" BOOK, IS THE CREDIT CARD LINE OF CREDIT

APPROACH. A HOUSE IS ON THE MARKET FOR $10,000 BADLY IN NEED OF REPAIR. YOU HAVE ALREADY APPLIED FOR 2 VISAS FROM 2 BANKS, WITH CREDIT LINES OF $5,000 EACH. YOU TAKE THE $10,000 AND PUT IT IN THE BANK. YOU THEN ATTEMPT TO GET THIS HOUSE AS CHEAPLY AS YOU CAN, SAY FOR $7,000. THE REMAINING $3,000 YOU USE FOR REPAIRS AND TO PAY THE MONTHLY VISA CHARGE. REMEMBER, DON'T BE LATE ON YOUR VISA PAYMENT IN THIS REGARD OR YOU WILL ONLY BE ABLE TO DO THIS ONCE. WITH THE HOUSE REHABILITATED, YOU EITHER PUT IT ON THE MARKET FOR A REASONABLE PRICE OR PUT A MORTGAGE ON IT AND KEEP IT AND RENT IT OUT. IF YOU DECIDE TO SELL, YOU HAD BETTER MAKE SURE THAT YOU HAVE NOT PUT TOO MUCH IN IT SO THAT YOU CAN PRICE IT SLIGHTLY BELOW MARKET FOR A FAST SALE.

REMEMBER, "FLIPPING," AS THIS IS CALLED, DEPENDS ON QUICK TURNOVER TIME AND A MINIMUM OF LONG TERM CARRYING COSTS. YOU HAVE THAT VISA PAYMENT TO MAKE, AND THE SOONER YOU FLIP THE PROPERTY AND INVEST THE PROFIT IN ANOTHER PROPERTY, THE QUICKER YOU WILL MAKE THAT MILLION BUCKS. REMEMBER TO

PUT AWAY SOME OF YOUR PROFITS FOR TAXES ON THE CAPITAL GAIN. IF YOU ARE SERIOUS ABOUT THIS TYPE OF REAL ESTATE INVESTING FOR ADDED OR PRIMARY INCOME, USE THE SERVICES OF AN ACCOUNTING PROFESSIONAL. YOU WILL SAVE YOURSELF A LOT OF GRIEF COME TAX TIME. BELIEVE ME, I KNOW. I WAS AUDITED BEFORE I KEPT GOOD RECORDS, AND IT WAS NO FUN SCRAPING UP RECEIPTS I SHOULD HAVE SAVED. THE I.R.S. AGENT I MIGHT SAY WAS VERY COOPERATIVE, AND I SURVIVED THIS WITHOUT OWING TOO MUCH. BUT HAD I KEPT BETTER RECORDS, I COULD HAVE DONE MUCH BETTER ON THE AUDIT.

ANOTHER WAY TO ACQUIRE PROPERTY IS TO LOOK FOR A PARTNER. DEPENDING ON YOUR FINANCIAL SITUATION, THIS MAY BE A PARTNER WITH ALL THE CASH OR ½ OF THE DOWN PAYMENT IN RETURN FOR YOUR "SWEAT EQUITY" TO MAKE UP YOUR HALF. I OWN PROPERTY WITH MY FATHER AND BROTHER, ONLY BECAUSE I DIDN'T HAVE ALL THE CASH I NEEDED TO BUY A PARTICULAR PROPERTY THAT I THOUGHT WAS HOT. RATHER THAN LOSE THE PROPERTY, I CUT THEM IN. THERE ARE MANY PROFESSIONALS IN YOUR AREA -DOCTORS, LAWYERS,

BUSINESSMEN, RETIRED FOLKS WHO ARE LOOKING FOR PROPERTIES TO INVEST IN BUT DO NOT HAVE THE TIME FOR MAINTENANCE OR DEALING WITH TENANTS, ETC. IF YOU ARE WILLING TO TAKE CARE OF THIS END IN RETURN FOR THEIR CAPITAL, YOU MAY HAVE A PARTNER. THE PAYOFF DEPENDS ON WHETHER YOU "FLIP" THE PROPERTY RIGHT AWAY OR HOLD ON TO IT FOR THE LONG TERM. THE FINANCIAL AGREEMENT YOU HAVE AS TO SPLITTING PROFITS COULD EASILY BE TAILORED TO WHATEVER YOU BOTH DESIRE. PUT IT IN WRITING AND DON'T WAIT UNTIL IT'S TIME TO SELL - DO IT WHEN YOU BUY. DON'T WAIT FOR MANY YEARS OF FALSE ASSUMPTIONS TO TAKE THEIR TOLL. AND IF YOU BUY PROPERTY WITH ANYONE OTHER THAN YOUR WIFE, CONSULT AN ATTORNEY SINCE THE TYPE OF TENANCY MENTIONED IN THE DEED COULD BE CRITICAL IF PROPERTY IS TO BE HELD ANY LENGTH OF TIME. THE PART OF YOUR PROPERTY YOU THOUGHT YOU WOULD AUTOMATICALLY INHERIT IF SOMETHING HAPPENED TO YOUR PARTNER COULD GO TO HIS HEIRS.

MOST OF ALL, MAKE FRIENDS WITH A GOOD, REASONABLE PLUMBER AND MAYBE AN

ELECTRICIAN. YOU MAY WANT TO BUY A PROPERTY WITH A TRADES PERSON WHO COULD DO THE REMODELING FOR AN AGREED UPON SHARE OF THE EVENTUAL PROFITS. THERE ARE MANY TRADESPEOPLE WHO MIGHT HAVE THE TIME TO DO THIS, ESPECIALLY WHERE ECONOMIES ARE SLOW.

Alan Ray Hoxie

BUYING INVESTMENT PROPERTY
DEALING WITH TENANT'S AND EVICTIONS
RENT PROGRAMS
WHERE THE DEALS ARE

YOU'VE COME THIS FAR IN THE BOOK AND ARE PROBABLY CONVINCED THAT YOU ARE NOT GOING TO LOOK FOR NO MONEY DOWN DEALS OR BUY A LOT OF TAPES WITH THAT VISA YOU JUST GOT. YOU ARE GOING TO LOOK FOR PARTNERS WITH CASH, AND YOU ARE GOING TO LOOK FOR PROPERTIES THAT NEED WORK, AND YOU ARE GOING TO PUT IN A GREAT DEAL OF YOUR OWN "SWEAT EQUITY" TO TURN A PROFIT.

ONE OF THE MOST COMMON AREAS WHERE DEALS CAN BE FOUND IS IN THE AREA OF ESTATES. IN THIS SITUATION, ESPECIALLY WHEN THE HOME NEEDS WORK AND A BANK WON'T MORTGAGE IT, YOU ARE MORE LIKELY TO OBTAIN A GOOD PRICE AND/OR A SHORT TERM BALLOON PAYMENT, ONE OR TWO YEARS, GIVING YOU ENOUGH TIME TO FIX IT UP AND FLIP IT. THE HEIRS OFTEN ARE OUT OF TOWN OR SIMPLY WANT OUT AND DO NOT WANT TO WORK ON THE HOME BECAUSE OF THE MEMORIES. THERE IS NO EASY WAY TO LOCATE ESTATES, BUT TO CONTACT

LAWYERS WHO DEAL HEAVILY IN REAL ESTATE IS A GOOD START. CONTACT THE SURROGATE JUDGE IN YOUR AREA, AND INFORM HIM/HER THAT YOU ARE IN THE MARKET FOR PURCHASING ESTATES. ALSO, CONTACT REAL ESTATE COMPANIES AND AGENTS.

I BOUGHT AN ESTATE FOR $30,000 WITH MY FATHER. WE PUT $5,000 DOWN, FIXED IT UP A BIT, KEPT IT FOR TWO YEARS AND SOLD IT FOR $47,500. ALL TOLD, WE DIDN'T INVEST MORE THAN $1,000 IN REPAIRS, BUT WE DID PUT TENANTS INTO THE HOME AND RENTS WERE AT MARKET VALUE.

YOU CAN ALSO LOOK TO FEDERAL FORECLOSURES. THESE DEALS REQUIRE MONEY DOWN AND THE FINANCIAL ABILITY TO CARRY THE APPROPRIATE MORTGAGE. LISTS OF FORECLOSURES OFFERED FOR SALE BY H.U.D. CAN BE OBTAINED AT MANY LOCAL REAL ESTATE OFFICES AND IN LOCAL PAPERS. MY OPINION, HOWEVER, IS THAT RECENTLY MANY OF THESE PROPERTIES HAVE BEEN APPRAISED TOO HIGH AND ARE NOT WORTH THE PRICE AT WHICH THEY ARE LISTED. IGNORE THE LISTING PRICE AND ONLY OFFER 50% OF THAT AND HOPE YOU MAKE A DECENT PROFIT. I'M NOT SURE WHETHER H.U.D. INFLATES THE LISTING PRICE AFTER THE APPRAISAL,

OR IF THE APPRAISERS ARE NOT PAYING ATTENTION TO THE AREAS AND CONDITIONS OF THESE HOMES, OR IF THERE IS AN OUTSTANDING MORTGAGE BALANCE TO COVER. BUT MOST OF THOSE I SEE ARE AT MARKET VALUE WHEN THEY SHOULD BE FAR BELOW.

TAKING THE FIRST STEP TOWARD OWNING INVESTMENT PROPERTY TAKES GUTS AND THE STICK-TO-IT-IVENESS TO SEE THE DEAL THROUGH AND THEN STAYING WITH THE PROPERTY ONCE IT'S YOURS. THE HEADACHES DON'T END ONCE YOU PURCHASE THE PROPERTY. THAT'S ONLY THE BEGINNING. YOU THEN HAVE TO MAKE IT WORK FOR YOU, AND THAT MEANS DEALING WITH TENANTS. MOST PEOPLE HAVE TROUBLE DEALING WITH THEIR KIDS AND THEIR IN-LAWS, LET ALONE WITH STRANGERS. THAT IS WHY THESE T.V. TAPES AND BOOKS SIT ON THE SHELF COLLECTING DUST. WHEN THE REALITY OF THE WORK INVOLVED SETS IN, MOST PEOPLE CONVENIENTLY FIND SOME OTHER DISTRACTION OR TURN ON THE TUBE, AND THE ONLY WINNER IS THE GUY SELLING TAPES TO SUCKERS IN TV LAND WHO CAN NO MORE AFFORD $400 FOR TAPES THAN THE MAN IN THE MOON. WE ARE A NATION OF

LOTTERY PLAYERS AND CHANNEL SURFERS. HOWEVER, FOR THOSE OF YOU NOT AFRAID OF WORK, LET'S GET INTO TENANT PROGRAMS AND DEALING WITH TENANTS.

THE SECTION 8 PROGRAM IS A FEDERALLY SUBSIDIZED PROGRAM OF RENT SUBSIDY AND IS AVAILABLE IN EVERY STATE. I USE THIS PROGRAM AS OFTEN AS I CAN FOR SEVERAL REASONS. YOUR RENT COMES DIRECTLY TO YOU, THE LANDLORD, BUT ONLY THE SUBSIDIZED PORTION. LET'S SAY THE RENT IS $500. SECTION 8 MAY PAY $300 BASED ON NEED, FAMILY SIZE, ETC., AND THE TENANT PAYS THE REST. THE TENANT IS USUALLY GOOD ABOUT PAYING THEIR SHARE BECAUSE THERE IS GENERALLY A WAITING PERIOD TO QUALIFY FOR THIS SUBSIDY, AND ONE OF THE FEW REASONS YOU CAN EVICT A TENANT IS FOR NON-PAYMENT OF THEIR SHARE. THEY WANT TO STAY ON THE PROGRAM. ONE KICKER, HOWEVER, IS THAT THE PROPERTY MUST CONFORM TO CERTAIN PHYSICAL STANDARDS SET BY H. U. D. THESE CONDITIONS, HOWEVER, ARE SIMILAR TO THE CODE REQUIREMENTS SET BY THE LOCALITY AND ARE NOT THAT HARD TO COMPLY WITH. THEY

ARE CALLED HQ's OR HOUSING QUALITY STANDARDS.

YOU SHOULD WANT TO KEEP YOUR PROPERTY IN GOOD SHAPE ANYWAY. ANOTHER PROGRAM FOR TENANTS RECEIVING SOCIAL SERVICE PAYMENTS IS THE RENT SUBSIDY PORTION OF SOCIAL SERVICES. THE TENANT CAN SIGN A VOUCHER THAT ENABLES A CERTAIN PORTION OF THEIR MONTHLY GRANT TO BE PAID DIRECTLY TO THE LANDLORD. I MENTION THESE PROGRAMS SINCE, IF YOU ARE GOING TO GO THE LOW MONEY DOWN OR LOW MONEY, TWO YEAR BALLOON APPROACH, YOU ARE GOING TO END UP WITH PROPERTIES IN AREAS WHERE THESE SOCIAL PROGRAMS FOR TENANTS ARE COMMON. IN BETTER AREAS, AN OWNER IS NOT GOING TO TRANSFER MONEY MAKING PROPERTY TO YOU FOR LITTLE MONEY DOWN.

TO BE A SUCCESSFUL LANDLORD, YOU MUST ALSO BE A SUCCESSFUL PSYCHOLOGIST, FATHER, AND BOSS. ONCE YOU RENT AN APARTMENT AND HAND OVER THE KEYS TO THE TENANT, THEY HAVE THE HAMMER AND THEY CAN BEAT YOU OVER THE HEAD, IF YOU THINK YOU'RE GOING TO PLAY "BIG, TOUGH GUY LANDLORD." I KNOW, I'VE PLAYED THIS

ROLE AND GOTTEN BEAT UP FINANCIALLY BY TENANTS. IN EVERY STATE, THERE ARE LOCAL LAWS THAT PROTECT THE RIGHTS OF TENANTS AND, BELIEVE ME, TENANTS KNOW MORE ABOUT TENANT-LANDLORD LAW THAN MOST LAWYERS. I HAD A JUDGE TELL ME THAT, AND I LAUGHED, BUT IT IS TRUE. TENANTS SPEND TIME IN HOUSING COURT WITH THEIR SOCIAL WORKER, WITH THE POLICE, AND THE LEGAL AID SOCIETY, AND IT DOESN'T COST THEM A CENT. IF YOU THINK YOU ARE GOING TO GET EVEN OR BROW BEAT AN UNCOOPERATIVE TENANT, YOU'RE WRONG. EVEN IF YOU EVICT THEM (AND AFTER ONE MONTH OF NONPAYMENT, I DO), THEY CAN DAMAGE A FEW WALLS, WINDOWS AND TOILETS ON THEIR WAY OUT. OF COURSE, IF YOU FIND THEM, YOU CAN SUE THEM, IF THEY HAVE SOMETHING FOR YOU TO RECOVER. I HAVE FOUND THE SECRET TO GOOD TENANT LANDLORD RELATIONS IS AS FOLLOWS:

1. TREAT YOUR PROPERTIES AS A BUSINESS. DON'T FALL IN LOVE WITH INANIMATE OBJECTS (HOUSES)
2. MAKE REPAIRS THAT ARE NECESSARY, MOST OF WHAT YOU REPAIR HAS BEEN BROKEN OR ABUSED BY TENANTS. IF THEY CAUSED DAMAGE, SEND A LETTER TELLING THEM THIS

WILL BE DEDUCTED FROM THE SECURITY DEPOSIT.
3. TREAT YOUR TENANTS LIKE A FATHER, BE STERN BUT FAIR AND CONVINCE THEM THAT YOU ARE PARTNERS IN THE MAINTENANCE AND OPERATION OF THE HOME. I ALLOW TENANTS TO SPEND UP TO $25 A MONTH ON UPGRADING AND REPAIRS AND DEDUCT IT FROM THEIR RENT. (ASK FOR RECEIPTS AND GIVE THEM NO CREDIT FOR LABOR.) DON'T FRATERNIZE OR GET TOO CHUMMY WITH YOUR TENANTS. REMEMBER, THIS IS YOUR BUSINESS, NOT A HOBBY.
4. SHOW YOUR TENANTS YOUR EXPENSES. I SHOW THEM MY MORTGAGE BOOKLET AND SHOW THEM WHAT I'M CHARGED FOR LATE PAYMENTS, AND I EXPLAIN THAT, AFTER ALL IS SAID AND DONE, I ONLY MAKE SO MUCH PROFIT PER MONTH, ETC. THEY APPRECIATE YOUR CONSIDERATION SINCE MOST TENANTS THINK LANDLORDS ARE WEALTHY CHEATS - SOME ARE, MOST ARE NOT.
5. ALWAYS FOLLOW LEGAL PROCEDURES AND GO THROUGH THE COURTS TO EVICT A TENANT. A MAN IN OUR CITY, ANGRY OVER A TENANT WHO OWED BACK RENT AND WAS, A CONSTANT PROBLEM TO HIM, CHANGED THE LOCKS AND PUT HER BELONGINGS TO THE CURB. THE LOCAL SCAVENGERS PROMPTLY HAULED AWAY HER TELEVISION SET, FURNITURE, ETC. SHE SUED THE LANDLORD, AND HE WAS ORDERED TO PAY HER $5,000 IN DAMAGES. TO EVICT HER PROPERLY WOULD HAVE COST HIM ABOUT $200.00 NOT TO MENTION THE BAD PRESS HE RECEIVED. THIS WAS ON THE FRONT PAGE OF THE METRO

SECTION. YOU CANNOT DO THINGS LIKE TURN OFF THE POWER OR HEAT, OR CHANGE THE LOCKS.

TENANTS ARE NOT DIRT OR SCUM, BUT PEOPLE WITH REAL PROBLEMS, REAL FAMILIES, AND REAL DREAMS. TREAT THEM AS A FATHER OR MOTHER OR EMPLOYER, AND BE AS FIRM AND FAIR AND CONSISTENT AS YOU CAN. NEVER GET INVOLVED IN INTER-TENANT SQUABBLES. THEY MUST BE MADE AWARE THAT THEY LIVE IN THE SAME BUILDING AND MUST WORK OUT THEIR OWN PROBLEMS. DO NOT GET INVOLVED IN THESE DOMESTIC DISPUTES. CONFINE YOUR CONCERN STRICTLY TO THE RENT AND THE LEASE TERMS.

DON'T BE FOOLED BY RACE OR EDUCATION OR OCCUPATION WHEN EVALUATING OR TRUSTING TENANTS. TO MAKE THINGS EASIER FOR YOURSELF, TRUST NO ONE. GET AT LEAST ONE MONTH SECURITY UP FRONT AND CHECK REFERENCES. DON'T RENT TO THE FIRST PERSON WHO HAPPENS BY. TAKE TIME TO INTERVIEW.

WHY IS THIS SECTION ON TENANTS SO IMPORTANT? AFTER YOU PURCHASE THAT "LOW DOWN PAYMENT" INCOME PROPERTY, YOU ARE GOING TO HAVE TO EFFECTIVELY DEAL WITH

TENANTS OR YOU WILL HAVE NOT ONLY NO CASH FLOW BUT NEGATIVE CASH FLOW IN REPAIRS AND BIG TROUBLE PAYING THE MORTGAGE. EVEN IF YOU BUY A PROPERTY TO IMMEDIATELY "FLIP" IT, IT MAY TAKE YOU A YEAR OR MORE TO EVENTUALLY UNLOAD THE PROPERTY FOR A PROFIT AND ALL DURING THAT TIME, YOU WILL BE DEALING WITH SOME SORT OF TENANT. PROPERTY, UNLIKE C.D.'S OR STOCK, IS NOT A LIQUID INVESTMENT AND MAY TAKE CONSIDERABLE TIME TO DISPOSE OF, EVEN AT A LOSS.

TO END THIS CHAPTER, AS I MENTIONED EARLIER, THE BEST DEALS ARE ESTATES, PROPERTIES BEING SOLD BECAUSE OF DIVORCE, TAX SALES BY MUNICIPALITIES, AND FEDERAL AND LOCAL BANK FORECLOSURES. BUT DO YOUR HOMEWORK, CHECK FOR PROPER USE IN ZONING, CODE VIOLATIONS AND LIENS ON THE PROPERTY.

I WANT TO TELL YOU A STORY ABOUT A DEAL I TRIED TO PUT TOGETHER SHOWING YOU HOW COMPLEX CERTAIN TRANSACTIONS CAN BECOME INVOLVING LIENS ON THE PROPERTY. A SUCCESSFUL BUSINESSMAN IN OUR TOWN CALLED ME TO FIND OUT THE HISTORY OF A PROPERTY HE HAD

PURCHASED BY QUIT CLAIM DEED. A QUIT CLAIM DEED, IN COMMON TERMS, IS A TRANSFER OF PROPERTY THAT SAYS, ESSENTIALLY, I DON'T KNOW WHAT I'VE GOT OR WHAT ENCUMBRANCES ARE ON THE PROPERTY, BUT WHATEVER IT IS, I'M TRANSFERRING IT TO YOU. THIS FELLOW, HOWEVER, DID NOT FILE HIS DEED WITH THE COUNTY, SO THERE WAS NO RECORD OF HIS OWNERSHIP. HE DID THIS BECAUSE HE WAS SURE THERE WERE LIENS AGAINST THE PROPERTY AND HE DIDN'T WANT TO ASSUME THEM. THIS WAS A VACANT LOT NEXT TO A GAS STATION, AND THE OIL COMPANY WANTED TO BUY IT FOR A CAR WASH. I CALLED A FRIEND OF MINE, WHO IS THE CITY ATTORNEY, AND HE RESEARCHED THE PROPERTY. THERE WAS A HOUSE ON IT AT ONE TIME THAT THE CITY DEMOLISHED. THE TOTAL LIEN AGAINST THE PROPERTY WAS ABOUT $20,000. NO WONDER HE DIDN'T WANT TO FILE HIS DEED. HOWEVER, SIX MONTHS AGO, THE CITY SOLD IT AT TAX AUCTION FOR $2,000. THE NEW OWNER WAS RELIEVED OF ALL THE BACK LIENS. I TOLD THE FIRST FELLOW THAT HE DID NOT OWN IT AND HE TURNED PALE, BUT, BEING A SMART BUSINESSMAN, HE KIND OF EXPECTED THIS. NOW THE GUY WHO BOUGHT IT

FOR $2,000 CAN SELL IT TO THE OIL COMPANY FOR BIG BUCKS!

WHEN PURCHASING A TWO OR THREE FAMILY HOME, IT IS IMPORTANT TO MAKE SURE THAT THE HOUSE IS PROPERLY ZONED. THIS IS ALSO CRUCIAL FOR A REAL ESTATE AGENT LISTING A HOME OF THIS TYPE. MANY OWNERS WILL ASSUME THAT BECAUSE THE HOME HAS ALWAYS HAD THAT IN-LAW RENTED THAT IT IS A LEGAL TWO FAMILY. NOT NECESSARILY SO.

IF THE OWNER IS NOT SURE OF THE ZONING AND YOU, THE AGENT, ARE NOT CONVINCED, SIMPLY CALL THE MUNICIPALITY AND ASK THEM FOR THE PROPER ZONING FOR THAT ADDRESS. BE ESPECIALLY SUSPICIOUS IF THE HOME HAS ONLY ONE FURNACE AND/OR ONE ELECTRIC METER. THE FIRST HOME I BOUGHT HAD THIS EXACT PROBLEM - A BEAUTIFUL UPSTAIRS IN-LAW APARTMENT THAT WAS DONE WITHOUT PERMITS OR ZONE CHANGES. WHEN THE BANK APPRAISER WALKED THROUGH THE HOUSE, HE MADE NOTE OF THIS. THE BANK REJECTED ANY MORTGAGE ON THE HOUSE BECAUSE IT WAS IMPROPERLY ZONED. THE OWNER WAS FORCED TO HOLD THE MORTGAGE. GOOD FOR ME! WHAT I

SUBSEQUENTLY DID WAS TO APPLY FOR A VARIANCE, WHICH WAS GRANTED, AND I SPLIT UP THE UTILITIES. I WAS THEN ABLE TO SELL IT LEGITIMATELY AS A TWO FAMILY. IF YOU ARE A REAL ESTATE AGENT, GET THIS STRAIGHTENED OUT AT THE BEGINNING BEFORE SPENDING TIME ON A HOME THAT BANKS WON'T MORTGAGE.

Alan Ray Hoxie

BUYING AND DEVELOPING LAND
AN OVERVIEW

THERE ARE GENERALLY TWO TYPES OF PEOPLE BUYING VACANT LAND. THE INDIVIDUAL HOPING ONE DAY TO BUILD A HOME ON THE PROPERTY OR THE LARGE DEVELOPER LOOKING TO PUT IN A SUBDIVISION OF HOMES. IN THE FIRST INSTANCE, AN INDIVIDUAL LOOKING TO BUY LAND HAS FEWER THINGS TO LOOK OUT FOR BUT, NONETHELESS, HAS SOME QUESTIONS TO ASK. FOR EXAMPLE, WHAT IS THE MINIMUM AMOUNT OF ACREAGE REQUIRED BY THE TOWN TO BUILD YOUR HOME? A SELLER WILL SELL YOU WHATEVER HE HAS FOR SALE, WHETHER IT'S BUILDABLE OR NOT. HE WANTS TO SELL AND IS NOT GOING TO ASK YOU WHAT YOU WANT TO DO WITH THE LAND. WHAT IS THE MINIMUM ROAD FRONTAGE REQUIRED? DOES THIS PARCEL COMPLY? WHAT IS THE ZONING ON THE PIECE? SAY YOU WANT TO HAVE HORSES. JUST BECAUSE THE PARCEL APPEARS TO BE "COUNTRY" DOESN'T MEAN BOARDING HORSES IS ALLOWED. WHAT TYPE OF UTILITIES ARE THERE? PUBLIC WATER AND SEWER OR WELL AND SEPTIC.

HOW CLOSE TO THE ROAD CAN YOU BUILD A HOME? THIS WILL, OF COURSE, DETERMINE THE COST OF YOUR DRIVEWAY AND INSTALLATION OF UTILITIES. MOST BANKS WILL NOT FINANCE VACANT LAND, SO YOU WILL HAVE TO WORK OUT A DEAL WITH THE SELLER EITHER ON A CASH DOWN MONTHLY PAY BASIS OR AN OPTION TO BE PAID OFF WHEN YOUR HOUSE IS COMPLETE AND OWNERSHIP TRANSFERRED. IF THE PROPERTY IS ON A HILL, CHECK WITH THE AUTHORITIES CONCERNING A "DRIVEWAY CUT." SOME PROPERTIES ARE SO CLOSE TO A HILL TOP THAT A DRIVEWAY IS NOT PERMITTED FOR SITE AND SAFETY PURPOSES. IF THIS IS THE CASE, AND YOU HAVE NOT ENOUGH FRONTAGE TO RELOCATE A DRIVEWAY, THE LAND COULD BE WORTHLESS. FIND THAT OUT BEFORE YOU BUY! IF YOU ARE BUYING A PARCEL TO SPLIT AFTER BUILDING YOUR DREAM HOME ON ONE SITE, MAKE SURE THAT SUBDIVIDING NOT ONLY IS POSSIBLE BUT INTO HOW MANY SALEABLE LOTS. THE LOCAL CODE ENFORCEMENT OFFICER OR ZONING ADMINISTRATOR CAN HELP YOU WITH THESE QUESTIONS. NEVER, NEVER ASSUME THAT THESE QUESTIONS ARE LITTLE PROBLEMS OR WILL GO AWAY. TOWN ZONING BOARD

AGENDAS ARE FILLED WITH CASES WHERE PEOPLE ASSUMED TOO MUCH AND GOT BURNED IN A PURCHASE OR ON AN ADDITION AND ARE NOW ASKING FOR RELIEF. ZONING BOARDS CAN BE TOUGH, MANY ARE, AND DO NOT LIKE TO GRANT VARIANCES LIKE CANDY. SAVE YOURSELF HEADACHES AND MONEY, DISCLOSE ALL YOUR INTENTIONS AND GET ANSWERS FROM THE SELLER OR THE TOWN IN WRITING TO YOUR SATISFACTION BEFORE YOU CLOSE ON THE PROPERTY.

AN EXAMPLE OF ASSUMING TOO MUCH IS TAKING PLACE IN A POSH RESORT TOWN TEN MILES FROM HERE AS I WRITE THIS. AN ATTORNEY HAD A FIRE IN HIS HOME WHILE HE WAS AWAY, AND THE HOME WAS GUTTED. AFTER HE BULLDOZED THE REMAINS INTO THE LAKE, HE REBUILT A HOME THREE TIMES LARGER THAN ZONING PERMITTED AND TOO CLOSE TO THE ROAD. THE ZONING BOARD CITED HIM AND THE LOCAL COURTS UPHELD THE CITATION. HE WAS ORDERED TO MOVE, FINED $ 100 A DAY, AND THE HOME WAS DEMOLISHED AND BILLED TO HIS PROPERTY TAXES. HE CLAIMS HE RECEIVED VERBAL PERMISSION FROM A ZONING OFFICER TO BUILD TO THAT SCALE. THE TOWN DENIES THAT, AND HE HAS

NO WRITTEN PROOF TO BACK HIM UP. ASSUME NOTHING AND GET ANSWERS IN WRITING.

IF THE PROPERTY IS NOT CLOSE TO PUBLIC WATER AND SEWERS, FIND OUT IF THE SOIL HAS BEEN "PERK TESTED" BY THE SELLER TO THE COUNTY'S SATISFACTION. "PERKED" MEANS PERCOLATION WHICH IS THE RATE AT WHICH THE GROUND ABSORBS WATER. THIS IS USUALLY THE DETERMINING FACTOR IN THE APPROVAL OF A SEPTIC SYSTEM. ASK NEIGHBORS OR A WELL DIGGER HOW DEEP THE WELLS ARE IN THE AREA. YOU WILL PAY BY THE FOOT AND AN 80 FT. WELL IS A LOT CHEAPER THAN ONE OF 200 FEET. ANOTHER IMPORTANT QUESTION IN PURCHASING RAW LAND IS HOW CLOSE TO THE SURFACE IS ROCK. IF VERY CLOSE, YOU MAY NOT BE ABLE TO HAVE A BASEMENT AND MAY HAVE TO GO WITH A RAISED RANCH OR OTHER ABOVE GROUND DESIGN. ARE THERE LANDFILLS NEARBY. ALTHOUGH TODAY THE GROUND WATER IS PRETTY WELL PROTECTED BY E.P.A. REGULATIONS, THE ODOR MAY BLOW DOWNWIND TOWARD YOUR PROPERTY. WHAT DOES THE ZONING OF THE AREA ALLOW TO BE BUILT NEXT TO YOU? IN OUR TOWN, A NURSERY MOVED INTO A

Alan Ray Hoxie

COUNTRY NEIGHBORHOOD AND THE NEIGHBORS WERE UP IN ARMS SAYING THEY NEVER KNEW THIS WAS PERMITTED. THIS HAS BEEN A PERMITTED USE FOR THAT AREA FOR TWENTY YEARS, EVEN THOUGH IT APPEARED TO BE RESIDENTIAL/COUNTRY. THE NURSERY TOOK OVER A FENCE COMPANY AND BOTH USES WERE GRANDFATHERED BY ZONING SINCE THERE WAS UNDER ONE YEAR OF NON-USE OF THE PROPERTY.

SUBDIVISIONS

THE DEVELOPMENT OF SUBDIVISIONS INTO SALEABLE LOTS SHOULD BE, AND USUALLY IS, ONLY UNDERTAKEN BY WELL-FINANCED BUILDERS OR OTHER EXPERIENCED INDIVIDUALS SUCH AS REAL ESTATE ATTORNEYS OR LARGE INVESTORS. A SUBDIVISION IS DEVELOPED ACCORDING TO THE STANDARDS SET UP BY THE MUNICIPALITY. BEFORE ANY SUBDIVISION IS APPROVED, MANY HOURS OF RESEARCH AND PLANNING ARE REQUIRED TO SATISFY THE CONCERNS OF THE LOCAL PLANNING BOARD. DRAINAGE CONCERNS ARE IDENTIFIED, STORM SEWER AND SANITARY SEWER DESIGNS APPROVED, AND WATER AND UTILITY PLANS OK'D. THERE ARE LITERALLY THOUSANDS OF DOLLARS SPENT ON ENGINEERING STUDIES AND PLANS, AND THOUSANDS DEPOSITED WITH THE TOWN AS SECURITY BEFORE A SHOVELFUL OF DIRT IS TURNED.

THE DEVELOPER IS RESPONSIBLE FOR THE COST OF ALL THESE IMPROVEMENTS AND, IN THE END, TURNS THEM OVER TO THE TOWN FOR THEIR MAINTENANCE FOR ETERNITY. THE DEVELOPER RECOUPS HIS EXPENSES ON LOT SALES TO BUILDERS AND, IF HE IS A BUILDER, ON EVENTUAL HOME SALES.

Alan Ray Hoxie

THIS IS WHY A LOT IN A SUBDIVISION IS THREE TO FOUR TIMES THE COST OF AN EQUIVALENT SIZE PIECE OF RAW LAND. THE MORE THE DEVELOPMENT COSTS. THE HIGHER THE PRICE OF THE LOTS WITHIN. CURRENTLY, MANY DEVELOPERS ARE GETTING HURT BECAUSE OF LAGGING HOME SALES. THEY STILL HAVE TO FINISH THE DEVELOPMENT WITHIN THE TIME CONSTRAINTS SET BY THE TOWN AND HAVE TO PAY ON MONEY BORROWED TO DO THIS. WHEN MONEY FROM LOT SALES SLOWS DOWN, SO DOES THEIR ABILITY TO CONTINUE DEVELOPMENT. MANY DEVELOPERS IN THE NORTHEAST ARE BEING HURT BECAUSE OF THIS PHENOMENON. ONE OF THE MAJOR COMPLAINTS OF MANY DEVELOPERS IS THAT THE TOWN IS TOO TOUGH IN MAINTAINING STANDARDS FOR DEVELOPMENTS. THE REASON IS THAT ONCE THE DEVELOPMENT IS TURNED OVER TO THE TOWN, REPAIR AND MAINTENANCE BECOME THE TOWN'S RESPONSIBILITY. NO MUNICIPALITY WANTS A SITUATION WHERE ROADS AND SEWERS START TO FALL APART WITHIN FIVE YEARS. THIS HAPPENS ALL OVER, ESPECIALLY WITH THE FREEZE AND THAW OF WINTER.

DEVELOPERS HAVE TO HAVE THEIR PLANS APPROVED BY THE LOCAL PLANNING BOARD. THE PLANNING BOARD, LIKE THE ZONING BOARD OF APPEALS, IS MADE UP OF USUALLY FIVE MEMBERS WHO ARE APPOINTED BY THE ELECTED TOWN BOARD OR CITY COUNCIL. ALTHOUGH MEMBERS OF THE PLANNING BOARD AND ZONING BOARD ARE ORDINARY CITIZENS, SOME REAL ESTATE OR PHYSICAL ENGINEERING EXPERIENCE IS DESIRABLE, ESPECIALLY ON THE PLANNING BOARD. BOTH BOARDS ARE USUALLY ASSISTED BY PROFESSIONAL COUNSEL, HOWEVER. THE PLANNING BOARD LOOKS AT THE WHOLE LAYOUT OF A SUBDIVISION, INCLUDING THE IMPACT OF DRAINAGE ON SURROUNDING AREAS, TRAFFIC FLOW INCREASES, STREET DESIGN, STORM BASIN SIZE, AND MANY OTHER AREAS CONTAINED IN A TOWN'S "MASTER PLAN." AN ENGINEERING FIRM IS CONTACTED TO ADDRESS ALL OF THE NECESSARY ISSUES BEFORE THE PLANNING BOARD IN AN ATTEMPT TO GAIN APPROVAL FOR THE START OF THE SUBDIVISION. AS I SAID EARLIER, MANY THOUSANDS OF DOLLARS ARE SPENT ON THESE PLANS BEFORE ONE SHOVELFUL OF DIRT IS TURNED AND THE APPROVAL TO BUILD IS

Alan Ray Hoxie

GRANTED. IN ADDITION, SEVERAL PUBLIC HEARINGS ARE HELD BY THE PLANNING BOARD TO RECEIVE AND ADDRESS CONCERNS OF NEIGHBORS WHO MAY BE IMPACTED. NOTICES ARE USUALLY MAILED TO NEARBY HOMEOWNERS, PUBLISHED IN THE LOCAL PAPER, AND EVEN STUCK ON TELEPHONE POLES, JUST LIKE IN COLONIAL DAYS.

NEW CONSTRUCTION (BUYING YOUR NEW HOME)

ONE THING THAT ALWAYS SURPRISES ME IS THE POPULAR TASTE FOR THE WORD "NEW." IN MY OPINION, THERE IS TOO MUCH SOCIAL PRESSURE SURROUNDING THE WORD AND TOO LITTLE VALUE. AS AMERICANS, HOWEVER, WE LOVE TO WALK INTO WORK AND TELL OUR BUDDIES THAT WE JUST BOUGHT A,"NEW" CAR WITH TREMENDOUS EMPHASIS ON THE "N" WORD. OUR WIVES OR GIRL FRIENDS JUST LOVE TO GO TO THAT WEDDING OR BABY SHOWER AND ANNOUNCE TO THE OTHERS THAT WE HAVE JUST STARTED TO BUILD OUR "NEW" HOUSE. THE ATTENTION AROUSED IS UNPARALLED IN MODERN HISTORY. IF A GUY GOES OUT AND BUYS A $30,000 CAR AND COMES BACK THE NEXT DAY TO TRADE IT IN, WHAT DO YOU THINK THEY WILL OFFER HIM: $20,000? REMEMBER, IT'S NOT "NEW" ANYMORE, IT'S USED. TAKE ANOTHER GUY WHO BUYS THAT $30,000 CAR TWO YEARS LATER FOR $18,000. WHO DO YOU THINK IS AHEAD? WHO WOULD YOU RATHER BE? I WOULD RATHER BE THE SECOND GUY WHO BUYS A CAR WITH A LOT OF LIFE LEFT IN IT. THEN I COULD

ALWAYS WALK AROUND AND TELL PEOPLE I BOUGHT IT "NEW" TWO YEARS AGO. YOU'LL GET THE SAME AMOUNT OF ATTENTION FOR A LOT LESS MONEY.

LET'S TALK ABOUT HOUSES. SAY YOU HAVE $200,000 TO SPEND ON A HOUSE, DO YOU THINK YOU CAN BUY MORE HOUSE AND PROPERTY NEW OR WITH A TEN YEAR OLD RESALE? IN MY EXPERIENCE, THE RESALE IS ALWAYS THE BETTER BUY THAN THE NEW HOME. LETS ASSUME FOR A MOMENT THAT YOU ARE NOT GOING TO ANY SHOWERS OR OTHER FUNCTIONS WHERE YOU CAN USE THE "N" WORD OVER AND OVER. WHAT ARE THE BENEFITS OF A NEW HOME? FIRST, THERE IS LOCATION THERE MAY NOT BE ANY RESALE HOMES IN THE AREA. SOME SUBDIVISIONS HOLD SO MUCH PRESTIGE THAT ANYONE WOULD BE CRAZY NOT TO WANT TO LIVE THERE. SECONDLY, IF YOU WANT A PARTICULAR DESIGN THAT IS NOT FOUND ELSEWHERE, YOU MAY HAVE TO BUILD NEW. THIRDLY, NEW HOMES ARE MORE ENERGY EFFICIENT SINCE ALL THE LATEST INSULATION, FURNACES, AND APPLIANCES ARE USED THAT WERE NOT AVAILABLE SAY TEN YEARS AGO. FOURTH IS YOU GET TO INVITE PEOPLE OVER TO SEE YOUR "NEW" HOME. THIS WILL ENHANCE YOUR SOCIAL LIFE. FIFTH, YOU GET TO BE

AN ACTIVE PARTICIPANT IN THE PURCHASE OF THAT $30,000 CAR THAT YOUR BUILDER WILL BUY HIS WIFE AFTER THE CLOSING. SIXTH AND LAST, ON A SERIOUS NOTE, NEW HOMES ARE DESIGNED FOR MORE MODERN LIFESTYLES WITH LARGER CLOSETS, CATHEDRAL CEILINGS, 2- I /2 OR MORE BATHS, DECKS, JACUZZI STYLE TUBS, AND SO ON. SOME OF THE DRAWBACKS, BY COMPARISON, OF NEW CONSTRUCTION ARE THAT YOU WILL HAVE TO DO MUCH OF THE LANDSCAPING YOURSELF, AND PROBABLY PUT IN A TARVIA DRIVEWAY AS WELL.

WHAT ABOUT THOSE COMMON NAIL POPS CAUSED BY THE WOOD SEASONING (NOT THE HOME SHIFTING OR SETTLING). WILL THE BUILDER COME BACK AND FIX THIS, OR WILL YOU BE CREDITED FOR FIXING THIS YOURSELF?

DO YOU WANT A FINISHED BASEMENT? IN A RESALE, YOU CAN PROBABLY FIND A NICELY FINISHED BASEMENT - USUALLY NOT IN NEW CONSTRUCTION. WILL THE BUILDER LET YOU DO SOME OF THE WORK YOURSELF OR HAVE A FRIEND IN THE TRADES HELP OUT? IT DOESN'T HURT TO ASK. I RECENTLY SOLD A HOUSE WHERE THE BUYER WAS A HEATING PROFESSIONAL AND HIS BROTHER A

PLUMBER. THE BUILDER ALLOWED HIM A CREDIT OF $7,000 TO DO THIS WORK HIMSELF, A JOB HE TOLD ME THEY COULD DO FOR ABOUT $4,000 OR LESS. HERE HE SAVED SOME MONEY, BUT THE BUILDER INSISTED THAT THEY WORK ACCORDING TO HIS TIMETABLE, WHICH WAS UNDERSTANDABLE. IN SOME STATES, THERE IS A ONE YEAR WARRANTY ON THE STRUCTURE OF THE HOUSE AND OTHER SEPARATE WARRANTIES ON THE FURNACE AND APPLIANCES, ACCORDING TO THE MANUFACTURER.

USUALLY THERE IS NOT MUCH ROOM FOR PRICE HAGGLING IN NEW CONSTRUCTION BECAUSE THE DEMAND IS STILL STRONGER THAN FOR RESALES. BUILDERS DO, HOWEVER, OFFER FINANCING INCENTIVES AND WILL OFTEN HELP WITH CLOSING COSTS OR BUY-DOWN MORTGAGES. AS IN ANYTHING IN LIFE, YOUR PRICE RANGE WILL DETERMINE WHAT EXTRAS YOU WILL GET WITH THE HOME. IF YOU ARE BUILDING NEW AT $125,000.00, EVERY LITTLE EXTRA WILL BE CHARGED TO YOU, YOU CAN BET.

HOWEVER, IF YOU ARE BUILDING NEW AT $900,000 YOU'LL GET ALL THE EXTRAS YOU WANT (IF YOU HAVEN,T ALREADY PAID FOR THEM IN THE PRICE).

AS FAR AS RESALES, GO, A HOME AS OLD AS 30 YEARS IS PROBABLY VERY SOUND AND SOMEWHAT UPDATED, YOU HAVE TO LOOK AT RESALES WITH AN EYE TOWARD WHAT YOU CAN DO YOURSELF AT CONSIDERABLE SAVINGS AS OPPOSED TO WHAT YOU WOULD PAY A BUILDER TO DO FOR YOU. MAYBE THE HOUSE YOU LOVE IS 30 YEARS OLD, SOLID, BUT THE ONLY DRAWBACK IS A SMALL MASTER BEDROOM. IS THAT SOMETHING YOU COULD EXPAND IN FUTURE YEARS? IF YOU,RE NOT SURE, CALL IN A CONTRACTOR TO GIVE YOU A PRICE ESTIMATE BEFORE YOU MAKE AN OFFER ON THE HOUSE. HOW MUCH WORK CAN YOU DO YOURSELF? THOSE WHO ARE WILLING TO PUT SOME "SWEAT EQUITY" INTO A HOME THAT NEEDS A LITTLE WORK ARE USUALLY FARTHER AHEAD THAN A BUYER WHO WANTS EVERYTHING DONE BY SOMEONE ELSE. RESALE HOMES ALSO ARE IN ESTABLISHED NEIGHBORHOODS WITH GROWN TREES, FOR EXAMPLE. IT MAY TAKE YEARS FOR NEW SUBDIVISIONS TO LOOK LIKE REAL NEIGHBORHOODS.

IF NEWER CONSTRUCTION IS STILL SOMETHING YOU DESIRE, LOOK FOR HOMES UNDER FIVE YEARS OLD THAT HAVE BEEN TAKEN OVER BY RELOCATION

COMPANIES. IN THIS INSTANCE, THE EMPLOYEE HAS BEEN TRANSFERRED OUT OF TOWN AND HAS BEEN GIVEN FAIR MARKET VALUE FOR THE HOUSE. THE RELOCATION COMPANY NOW OWNS THE HOME AND MAY BE MORE CONSIDERATE OF A LOW OFFER BECAUSE THERE IS NO EMOTIONAL TIES THAT EXIST AND THEIR MAIN CONCERN IS TO MOVE THE PROPERTY WITHOUT INCURRING TOO MANY OTHER CARRYING EXPENSES SUCH AS UTILITIES, TAXES, ETC.

IN TODAY'S MARKET, THERE ARE MANY NEARLY NEW HOMES THAT ARE SELLING BELOW WHAT IT COST FIVE YEARS AGO TO BUILD THEM. DON'T GET HUNG UP ON "NEW" WITHOUT CONSIDERING THOSE FIVE YEAR OLD GEMS.

MORTGAGES

THERE ARE MANY DIFFERENT TYPES OF MORTGAGES AVAILABLE TODAY. MOST COMMONLY, FIXED RATE AND ADJUSTABLE RATE LOANS. BANKS INVENTED THE ADJUSTABLE MORTGAGE TO PROTECT THEIR CASH FLOW THROUGH CHANGING TIMES. OUR LIFESTYLES ALSO HAVE DICTATED THE DEVELOPMENT OF DIFFERENT MORTGAGE OPTIONS. SOMEONE WHO IS FAIRLY CONFIDENT THAT THEY WILL BE IN THEIR HOME FIVE YEARS OR LESS PROBABLY WON'T GET HURT WITH AN ADJUSTABLE RATE MORTGAGE. ON THE OTHER HAND, IF THIS NEXT MOVE IS YOUR LAST, I WOULD RECOMMEND LOOKING AT THE LOWEST POSSIBLE FIXED RATE EVEN IF I HAD TO PAY MORE IN POINTS TO GET IT. WHAT IS A POINT? A POINT IS ONE PERCENT OF THE AMOUNT YOU WISH TO MORTGAGE, NOT ONE PERCENT OF THE PURCHASE PRICE OR ANYTHING ELSE. THIS THE BANK CHARGES YOU FOR THE PRIVILEGE OF GIVING YOU THE LOWER RATE. THEY GET IT UP FRONT IN POINTS RATHER THAN OVER 20 OR 30 YEARS. THERE ARE BUY DOWN MORTGAGES. THIS IS A NEWER TYPE OF LOAN WHERE FOR A PRICE

UP FRONT YOU GET A FIXED RATE MORTGAGE WHERE THE FIRST COUPLE OF YEARS ARE AT A LOWER RATE THAN NORMAL. THIS LOAN ALLOWS A BUYER TO QUALIFY FOR MORE HOUSE AT THE LOWER FIRST YEAR RATE. IT MAY THEN GRADUALLY RISE A COUPLE PERCENT OR REMAIN FIXED, DEPENDING ON THE PROGRAM. WHAT ABOUT V.A. OR F.H.A., VETERANS ADMINISTRATION LOANS ARE FINE TO USE, PROVIDING YOU WERE IN THE SERVICE, OF COURSE, AND PROVIDING THE RATE IS SUBSTANTIALLY LESS THAN THE NORMAL RATE. WITH NORMAL RATES QUITE LOW RIGHT NOW, THERE REALLY IS NO GREAT REASON FOR ANYONE TO GO FOR A V.A. LOAN. THEY DO TAKE LONGER TO CLOSE AND, IF THE RATES ARE NOT LESS THAN PREVAILING, I DON'T SEE THE ADVANTAGE. THE F.H.A. LOANS ARE BACKED AND FUNDED BY THE FEDERAL DEPARTMENT OF H.U.D. THERE ARE CEILINGS ON INCOME AND HOME PURCHASE PRICE AND THERE ARE CREDIT LIMITATIONS AND DEBT TO INCOME RATIOS.

HOW ABOUT REFINANCING? LAST YEAR I HAD SOME CUSTOMERS WHO WANTED TO MOVE, BUT ALSO WANTED TO CONSOLIDATE SOME DEBTS INTO A

TAX DEDUCTIBLE SITUATION. THESE FOLKS WOULDN'T LOWER THE PRICE OF THEIR HOME, SO I SUGGESTED THAT THEY STAY WHERE THEY WERE (THEY WOULD HAVE ANYWAY AT THAT HIGH PRICE) AND REFINANCE SINCE THEIR EQUITY WAS ABOUT $50,000. THIS IS WHAT THEY DID AND PAID OFF CAR LOANS, ETC., AND NOW HAVE ONLY ONE LARGER MORTGAGE PAYMENT WHICH STILL IS LESS BY ABOUT $200 A MONTH THAN THE SUM OF ALL THE OTHER SMALLER LOANS TOTALED. THE RULE OF THUMB THAT EVERY REAL ESTATE COLUMNIST HAS PUBLISHED HUNDREDS OF TIMES IS THAT YOU SHOULD ONLY REFINANCE IF YOU CAN GET A MORTGAGE AT LEAST TWO PERCENTAGE POINTS LESS THAN THE CURRENT MORTGAGE AND WHAT IT COSTS YOU TO REFINANCE CAN BE RECOVERED IN FIVE YEARS AND, OF COURSE, IF YOU PLAN TO STAY IN THE HOME FIVE YEARS OR LONGER. IF YOU ARE TAKING CASH OUT WHEN YOU REFINANCE, I WOULD SUGGEST THAT A RULE OF THUMB THERE IS TO TAKE ENOUGH TO JUSTIFY THE REFINANCING COSTS. FOR EXAMPLE, IF IT COSTS YOU $2,500 TO REFINANCE, IT WOULD BE PRUDENT TO TAKE OUT AT LEAST $5,000 TO USE FOR OTHER PURPOSES SINCE NOW YOUR

INTEREST RATE AND MONTHLY PAYMENT ARE LESS THAN BEFORE. IN THE IMMORTAL WORDS OF ARISTOTLE ONASSIS, "ALWAYS BORROW AS MUCH AS YOU CAN, ALWAYS PAY IT BACK ON TIME, AND ALWAYS HAVE A TAN."

IF YOU WANT TO REFINANCE INCOME PROPERTY OR BUSINESS PROPERTY TO GET CASH OUT, YOU MAY NOT FIND A SOURCE THAT PERMITS THIS. MANY BANKS, SINCE THE S&L CRISIS, HAVE STOPPED ALLOWING CASH OUT REFINANCES ON A NON-OWNER OCCUPIED PROPERTY, INVESTORS TAKING CASH OUT AND WALKING AWAY FROM PROPERTY AFTER A REFINANCE WAS ANOTHER REASON FOR THE S&L CRISIS, ALONG WITH BAD APPRAISALS.

BEFORE YOU START LOOKING FOR A HOME, I WOULD SUGGEST YOU CALL A BANK OR MORTGAGE BROKER AND SIT DOWN WITH A REPRESENTATIVE TO BE QUALIFIED AS TO THE AMOUNT OF THE MORTGAGE YOU ARE LIKELY TO BE GIVEN. MANY REAL ESTATE AGENTS CAN DO THIS AS WELL AS MORTGAGE BROKERS, BUT THE TRUTH IS THAT THERE ARE SO MANY INDIVIDUALS WITH REAL ESTATE LICENSES, BOTH FULL AND PART TIME, THAT YOU WOULD BE BETTER SERVED WITH A MORTGAGE

BROKER. I RECOMMEND IT BECAUSE OF THEIR INCREASED ACCURACY AND AVAILABILITY OF CREDIT CHECKING RESOURCES ON SITE. I SEND ALL MY CUSTOMERS TO MORTGAGE BROKERS FOR QUALIFYING BEFORE I BEGIN WORKING WITH THEM. THEIR CREDIT IS CHECKED, INCOME AND DEBTS VERIFIED, AND WE ARE MORE CONFIDENT OF THE RANGE OF PRICE WE SHOULD STAY WITHIN. THIS ALSO FACILITATES THE CLOSING PROCESS SINCE MUCH OF THE INITIAL PAPERWORK IS ALREADY DONE. HERE ARE MOST OF THE ITEMS THAT A BANK OR MORTGAGE BROKER WANTS TO SEE TO PROPERLY QUALIFY YOU:

1. CREDIT CARD NUMBERS, ADDRESSES, AND APPROXIMATE BALANCES.
2. BANK ACCOUNT, NUMBERS, ADDRESSES AND BALANCES.
3. ALL OTHER LOANS, NUMBERS, ADDRESSES AND BALANCES.
4. IF SELF EMPLOYED, TWO YEARS TAX RETURNS.
5. LATEST PAY STUBS.
6. MONEY IN THE BANK, OR GIFT LETTER, IN SUFFICIENT AMOUNT TO COVER DOWN PAYMENT AND CLOSING COSTS.
7. IRA STATEMENTS.
8. VERIFICATION OF EMPLOYMENT AND LENGTH OF EMPLOYMENT.

BORROWING MONEY FROM A CREDIT UNION, IF MONEY IS NEED TO CLOSE, IS A GOOD IDEA SINCE THESE LOANS DON'T NORMALLY SHOW UP ON A CREDIT CHECK. IF THE LOAN DOESN'T SHOW UP, IT WILL NOT BE CALCULATED IN YOUR DEBT LOAD. THE CREDIT UNION LOAN FOR CLOSING COSTS OR A DOWN PAYMENT CAN BE PAID BACK OVER TIME OR BY YOUR TENANTS FROM YOUR MONTHLY CASH FLOW. ESTABLISH A RELATIONSHIP WITH A CREDIT UNION AND USE IT. YOU'LL FIND FAIR LOAN RATES THERE AND MORE PERSONAL SERVICE, IN MANY CASES.

THERE HAS BEEN A GREAT DEAL OF PROMOTION OF THE BI-WEEKLY FIFTEEN YEAR MORTGAGE. SOME OF THE PLUSES OF THIS MORTGAGE ARE THAT IS PAID OFF MORE QUICKLY THAN A 30-YEAR LOAN AND YOU PAY CONSIDERABLY LESS IN INTEREST. HOWEVER, IN THESE TIMES OF FEWER TAX DEDUCTIONS, ONE OF THE FEW REMAINING DEDUCTIONS WE HAVE IS ON OUR MORTGAGE INTEREST. BY THE TIME YOUR MORTGAGE, IN FIFTEEN YEARS, IS PAID OFF, YOU MAY DESPERATELY NEED THAT TAX DEDUCTION. WHAT DO YOU DO THEN? REFINANCE AND USE THE

CASH FOR SOMETHING, CASH GENERATING OR DEDUCTIBLE, WHAT ELSE?

YOU CAN ACCOMPLISH ALMOST THE SAME THING WITH A 30-YEAR MORTGAGE BY MAKING ONE EXTRA PAYMENT PER YEAR TO BE APPLIED DIRECTLY TO PRINCIPAL. WHEN YOU SEND THAT PAYMENT IN, EQUAL TO YOUR MONTHLY PAYMENT, SENT A NOTE THAT SPECIFICALLY SAYS "APPLY TO PRINCIPAL, EXTRA PAYMENT. " THIS WAY IS MORE FLEXIBLE SINCE YOU ACCOMPLISH NEARLY THE SAME THING AS A BI-WEEKLY MORTGAGE BUT HAVE THE FLEXIBILITY OF RETURNING TO THE LOWER PAYMENT IF THINGS GET TIGHT. IN THESE TROUBLED TIMES OF DOWNSIZING AND LAYOFFS, I WOULD WANT TO HAVE THE FLEXIBILITY OF THE LATER PROPOSAL. IF YOU PLAN ON MOVING QUITE A BIT, SAY EVERY FIVE YEARS OR LESS, YOU MAY WANT TO LOOK INTO AN ASSUMABLE MORTGAGE, GENERALLY F.H.A. OR V.A. THE ASSUMABILITY FEATURE IS AN ASSET SINCE YOU WON'T HAVE A WHOLE LOT OF EQUITY BUILT UP. YOU MAY BE ABLE TO SELL QUICKER NO MATTER WHAT THE MARKET IS LIKE AND FOR AN AMOUNT CLOSER TO YOUR ASKING PRICE. ASSUMABILITY IS ALWAYS AN ASSET EXCEPT

WHERE YOU HAVE A LARGE EQUITY BUILD UP. NOBODY WALKS AROUND WITH A LOT OF CASH IN POCKET TO ASSUME A MORTGAGE. IF YOU HAVE AN ASSUMABLE MORTGAGE AND ARE LEAVING TOWN, IT WOULD BE WISE TO BE RELEASED FROM ANY FURTHER OBLIGATION ONCE YOUR MORTGAGE IS ASSUMED. OTHERWISE, IF YOUR BUYER DEFAULTS, SOMEONE WILL BE LOOKING FOR YOU TO TAKE OVER THE LOAN. ANY ATTORNEY CAN HELP YOU EXECUTE THE RELEASE FORMS ON AN ASSUMPTION. HOWEVER, IF YOU WANT TO BE RELEASED FROM LIABILITY, THE LOAN BECOMES CONDITIONALLY ASSUMABLE, NOT FULLY ASSUMABLE. REMEMBER TO SHOP AROUND BEFORE YOU COMMIT TO ONE BANK OR MORTGAGE BROKER. (I CALL FOUR OR FIVE SOURCES I USE REGULARLY AND USUALLY GO WITH WHOMEVER HAS THE LOWEST RATE FOR THE FEWEST POINTS. THERE CAN BE QUITE A DIFFERENCE IN RATES VERSUS POINTS FROM BANK TO BANK, SO IT PAYS - MAYBE SEVERAL HUNDRED DOLLARS - TO SHOP AROUND.

WHAT ARE CLOSING COSTS AND WHAT DO THEY COST? THESE COSTS VARY FROM STATE TO STATE, EVEN COUNTY TO COUNTY, BUT I WILL SAY THAT A

RULE OF THUMB IS THAT CLOSING COSTS, EXCLUSIVE OF POINTS, GENERALLY RUN FIVE PERCENT OF THE MORTGAGE AMOUNT. AS THE BUYER, YOU PAY FOR ALL THE COSTS THE BANK INCURS FOR CHECKING THE PROPERTY AGAINST OUTSIDE INTERESTS AND LIENS OR ANYTHING THAT WOULD INFRINGE ON THE BANK'S ABILITY TO SAFELY OWN YOUR PROPERTY WITH YOU AS ITS PARTNER. YOU PAY FOR THE BANK'S ATTORNEY AND FOR ALL THE PAPERWORK THE ATTORNEY REVIEWS - ABSTRACT, UPDATES, SURVEYS, PREPAID PROPERTY TAXES, AND THE ATTORNEY'S PERSONAL FEE. THAT IS WHY I RECOMMEND ON A REFINANCE TO USE THE BANK'S LAWYER AS YOUR OWN SINCE THE REVIEW OF THE PAPERWORK IS IDENTICAL. IN MOST CASES, SINCE YOU ARE ALREADY PAYING HIM TO DO IT FOR THE BANK, THE ATTORNEY WILL CHARGE YOU VERY LITTLE OR NOTHING ADDITIONAL TO REPRESENT YOU SINCE IT IS REASONABLE TO ASSUME THAT WHEN YOU SELL YOU WILL USE THAT FIRM AS ATTORNEY AS THEY ALREADY HAVE THE PAPERWORK FROM THE REFINANCE. THE BANK HAS A LARGER STAKE IN THE PROPERTY THAN YOU DO AND, SINCE A REFINANCE IS NOT A CHANGE IN DEED OR TITLE USUALLY, IT'S NOT

AS RISKY A PROCEDURE AS AN OUTRIGHT SALE AND TRANSFER OF OWNERSHIP. THE LAST TWO REFINANCES I DID I USED THE BANK'S ATTORNEY AS MY ATTORNEY, AND HE CHARGED ME NOTHING AT ALL OVER AND ABOVE WHAT I WOULD HAVE PAID TO HIM AS ATTORNEY FOR THE BANK.

I FEEL IT IS IMPORTANT TO SAY, ESPECIALLY IN THESE TROUBLED TIMES, THAT IF YOU ARE HAVING DIFFICULTY PAYING YOUR MORTGAGE PAYMENTS OR PAYING ON TIME, COMMUNICATE WITH YOUR BANK AND EXPLAIN THE SITUATION, DON'T JUST RUN AWAY OR BURY YOUR HEAD IN THE SAND. BANKS DON'T WANT TO OWN REAL ESTATE; THEY DON'T WANT TO SELL REAL ESTATE. THEY'RE SMARTER THAN THAT. THEY WANT TO LEND MONEY AND MAKE MONEY ON WHAT THEY LEND. MOST LENDERS ARE SYMPATHETIC TO WHAT IS GOING ON IN TODAY'S ECONOMY AND WILL DO ALL THEY CAN TO WORK WITH YOU IN TOUGH TIMES, BUT YOU'VE GOT TO INITIATE THE CONVERSATION, EXPLAIN YOUR PROBLEM, AND STICK TO AN ARRANGED PAYMENT SCHEDULE.

ON A FIXED RATE MORTGAGE, YOU MAY SEE YOUR PAYMENT RISE OVER THE YEARS. THE REASON

FOR THAT MAY BE THAT YOUR PROPERTY TAXES HAVE GONE UP AND THE BANK IS PASSING THAT ALONG TO YOU IN HIGHER PAYMENTS. ANOTHER REASON FOR THE INCREASE COULD BE THAT BECAUSE OF THE PROPERTY TAX INCREASE, THE BANK MAY TAKE MORE FROM YOU EACH MONTH BUT WILL THEN REDUCE YOUR PAYMENT SOMEWHAT AFTER THE ESCROW ACCOUNT HELD BY THEM TO PAY YOUR TAXES HAS ENOUGH MONEY IN IT TO PREPAY YOUR TAXES FOR A PERIOD OF TIME. IN ANY EVENT, YOU SHOULD CONTACT THE BANK ONCE A YEAR AND ASK FOR AN ESCROW ACCOUNT REVIEW IF YOUR MONTHLY PAYMENTS ON A FIXED RATE MORTGAGE HAVE INCREASED. THE ATTORNEY GENERAL IN A NORTHEASTERN STATE HANDLED A CLASS ACTION SUIT AGAINST SOME BANKS WHO HAD TAKEN TOO MUCH THIS WAY, AND THE MONEY WAS RETURNED TO THE HOMEOWNERS AND PAYMENTS SUBSEQUENTLY LOWERED.

WHAT IS AN ADJUSTABLE RATE MORTGAGE AND WHAT ARE ITS BENEFITS?

THIS MORTGAGE IS USUALLY MORE BENEFICIAL FOR THOSE WHO PLAN ON MOVING FREQUENTLY BECAUSE OF JOB TRANSFERS OR AGE. HOLDERS OF

THESE MORTGAGES HAVE BEEN DOING WELL WITH LOW RATES FOR THE PAST TEN YEARS BECAUSE MARKET INTEREST RATES, WITH WHICH THEY ARE TIED, HAVE NOT GONE UP MUCH. AN EXAMPLE IS A THREE YEAR ADJUSTABLE RATE AT SIX PERCENT. AFTER THAT, THEY MENTION A CAP OF SAY ONE PERCENT. THIS MEANS THAT EVERY THREE YEARS, IF INTEREST RATES HAVE GONE UP, NO MATTER HOW HIGH, YOUR RATE CAN ONLY BE RAISED ONE PERCENT AND ONLY ON THE THIRD ANNIVERSARY. THE LAST ITEM YOU THEN READ ABOUT IS A LIFETIME CAP OF, FOR EXAMPLE, FIVE PERCENT. THIS MEANS THAT FOR THE LIFE OF THE MORTGAGE, LET'S SAY 30 YEARS, THE HIGHEST YOUR MORTGAGE INTEREST COULD BE IS ELEVEN PERCENT, NO HIGHER. IF RATES GO DOWN, YOUR MORTGAGE RATE WILL MOST LIKELY STAY AT 6% AND NOT DECREASE.

AS AN INVESTOR, YOU SHOULD FIND A BANK OR MORTGAGE LENDER WHO IS WILLING TO MORTGAGE NON-OWNER OCCUPIED PROPERTY AND DEVELOP A GOOD RELATIONSHIP WITH THAT SOURCE. THE MORE SINGLE INDIVIDUAL RELATIONSHIPS YOU HAVE WITH PRIVATE INVESTORS HOLDING MORTGAGES, THE MORE PROPERTY YOU ARE LIKELY TO ACCUMULATE.

THE SHORTER THE TIME LIMIT YOU ASK A SELLER TO HOLD THE MORTGAGE, THE MORE PROPERTY YOU CAN PURCHASE AT A HIGHER QUALITY SINCE THE EVENTUAL PAYOFF IS SOONER. TO DO THIS, YOU MUST KNOW THAT THERE WILL BE A BANK IN THE WINGS TO BACK YOU UP WHEN THE BALLOON MORTGAGE POPS.

WHEN YOU NEGOTIATE WITH A SELLER FOR A PROPERTY YOU WANT, IT IS ADVISABLE TO HAVE A LOCAL REAL ESTATE ATTORNEY WITH WHOM TO CONFER. A CRITICISM I HAVE WITH ALL THESE NO-MONEY DOWN TELEVISION TAPES IS THAT THEY TRY TO BE ALL THINGS TO ALL PEOPLE AND END UP BEING SO GENERIC THAT THEY ARE USELESS. THE REAL ESTATE MARKET METHODS OF PURCHASING AND CLOSING PROCEDURES ARE VERY DIFFERENT IN CALIFORNIA FROM THE NORTHEAST. YOU MAY BE SAYING THINGS TO A SELLER THAT YOU HEARD ON A TAPE THAT HAVE NO MEANING OR RELEVANCE IN CONNECTICUT OR NEW YORK.

IN CLOSING THIS CHAPTER, REMEMBER THAT YOU CANNOT BE AN ISLAND AND BE SUCCESSFUL IN REAL ESTATE INVESTING. YOU HAVE TO GO OUT AND MEET SELLERS, MEET ATTORNEYS WHO WILL HELP YOU,

AND MEET BANKERS OR OTHER LENDERS WHO CAN BACK UP YOUR DREAMS WITH LOANS. THE REASON THAT SO MANY PEOPLE DO NOT FOLLOW THROUGH ONCE THEY ORDER THESE NO-MONEY DOWN TAPES IS SIMPLY THAT IT INVOLVES WORK AND INVOLVES RISKS. THERE IS ONLY A SMALL PERCENTAGE OF AMERICANS WHO WILL TAKE THESE RISKS AND ASSUME THE WORK AND RESPONSIBILITY THAT GOES WITH IT. IT IS FAR EASIER TO ORDER TAPES OVER THE PHONE WITH YOUR CREDIT CARD AND SIT AND DREAM OF ALL THE PROPERTY YOU SOMEDAY WILL CONTROL, IF YOU GET AROUND TO IT. DON'T LET THE SPECTER OF PURCHASING PROPERTY OVERWHELM YOU. START SMALL AND START SLOW. YOU NEED A THOROUGH UNDERSTANDING OF REAL ESTATE TO STAY IN THE RING, AND YOU MUST TAKE PURCHASING EACH PROPERTY ONE STEP AT A TIME. ONCE YOU MAKE THAT DECISION TO BUY, STAY WITH IT. A CHINESE PHILOSOPHER ONCE SAID THAT A JOURNEY OF 1000 MILES BEGINS WITH A SINGLE STEP.

I HAVE NEVER PURCHASED A PROPERTY I REGRETTED BUYING, EVEN WHEN PRESENTED WITH SUBSTANTIAL HEADACHES IN MANAGING IT. YOU HAVE TO BELIEVE THAT REAL ESTATE IS THE BEST

INVESTMENT YOU CAN MAKE OR YOU'RE THROUGH. I AM CONVINCED THAT IT IS, BUT ONLY FOR THE LONG TERM AND ONLY WITH CONTINUED VIGILANCE TOWARD GOOD TENANT RELATIONSHIPS AND ADEQUATE PROPERTY MAINTENANCE. DON'T BUY A HOUSE THINKING YOU'LL FLIP IT AND BUY A BOAT. BUY A PROPERTY WITH THE INTENT OF HAVING THE MORTGAGE PAID OFF BY THE TENANTS IN 10 OR 20 YEARS AND THEN REFINANCING IT TO PAY FOR YOUR DAUGHTER'S COLLEGE TUITION AND CONTINUE TO LET THE TENANTS PAY OFF THAT MORTGAGE. THIS IS THE REAL BENEFIT OF REAL ESTATE OWNERSHIP. IT IS LONG TERM AND NOT EASILY LIQUID. START SMALL, BUY A TWO FAMILY, LEARN HOW TO DEAL WITH TENANTS, LEARN A LITTLE ABOUT PLUMBING, CARPENTRY, ETC., THEN GO ON TO PURCHASE ANOTHER PROPERTY WHEN YOUR CONFIDENCE AS A LANDLORD IS BUILT UP. GOING AFTER TOO MUCH TOO SOON WILL OVERWHELM YOU, SCARE YOU, PROBABLY COST YOU, AND MAY DRIVE YOU AWAY FROM PROPERTY ACQUISITION FOREVER. HOWEVER, THIS IS COMPLETELY OPPOSITE FROM WHAT THE GUYS ON T.V. SAY. ACCORDING TO THEM, IN A SHORT TIME FOR VERY LITTLE MONEY, YOU WILL BE ABLE

TO QUIT YOUR DAY JOB AND BE INTERVIEWED IN HAWAII WITH A SUPERB, POSITIVE CASH FLOW. DON'T BET ON IT AND DON'T QUIT YOUR DAY JOB!

YOU MAY WANT TO LOOK AT 2 FAMILY HOMES FOR YOUR FIRST HOME SINCE THE MONTHLY COST IS OFFSET BY THE RENT RECEIVED, AND YOU WILL LEARN TO DO SMALL REPAIRS THAT HOME OWNERSHIP INVOLVES. THEN, WHEN YOU DECIDE TO MOVE ON, YOU COULD KEEP THE 2 FAMILY AND USE MONEY SAVED FOR THE CLOSING AND DOWN PAYMENT ON ANOTHER HOME OR SELL AND USE THE EQUITY AS A DOWN PAYMENT. OBVIOUSLY, THE BENEFIT TO KEEPING THE 2 FAMILY IS THAT YOU KNOW THE HOUSE AND WHAT YOU HAVE REPAIRED OR UPDATED. YOU BENEFIT FROM THE TAX WRITE OFFS AND YOU HAVE THAT BUILT-IN CASH FLOW AND A PROPERTY TO REFINANCE FOR YOUR RETIREMENT OR A CHILD'S COLLEGE EDUCATION. IF YOU CAN QUALIFY FOR THAT MOVE-UP HOME AND STILL KEEP THE 2 FAMILY, I WOULD SAY KEEP IT. IF NOT, AS DETERMINED BY THE LENDER, YOU WILL HAVE TO SELL. MY FIRST HOME WAS A 2 FAMILY IN A MARGINAL AREA OF OUR CITY. THE HOUSE WAS NOT THAT OLD AND HAD POTENTIAL. I BOUGHT IT FOR

$25,000.00, RECEIVED RENT ON THE UPPER UNIT FOR THE 4 YEARS I OWNED IT, AND SOLD IT IN 1985 FOR A $29,000 PROFIT. THIS I USED FOR A DOWN PAYMENT ON THE HOME I NOW OCCUPY. A PLACE THAT NEEDED WORK, BUT HAS A BEAUTIFUL VIEW AND IT WAS WHAT I WAS LOOKING FOR, A 3 BEDROOM, 2 CAR GARAGE RANCH STYLE HOME. DON'T BE AFRAID OF A HOME THAT NEEDS WORK. THIS IS WHERE THE REAL BUYS ARE. YOU CAN DO THE UPDATING AND REPAIRS AS YOU LIVE IN THE HOME AND WHEN YOU HAVE SOME EXTRA MONEY. FORECLOSURE PROPERTIES ARE AMONG THIS GROUP. REAL ESTATE COMPANIES AND ANY MUNICIPAL TAX DEPARTMENT HAVE LISTS OF THESE PROPERTIES. THE CHAPTER ON AUCTIONS WILL ALSO GIVE MORE DETAIL ABOUT THAT AVENUE. THE LONG AND SHORT OF THE WHOLE PROCESS IS TO HAVE YOUR CREDIT STRAIGHTENED OUT AND YOUR FINANCING LIMITS SET BEFORE YOU GO SHOPPING. IN THIS WAY, YOU WILL NOT LOSE THE HOME OF YOUR DREAMS BY NOT QUALIFYING AFTER HAVING AN OFFER ACCEPTED.

WHEN YOU DECIDE TO GO HOME SHOPPING, LET EVERYONE KNOW YOU ARE IN THE MARKET. I FOUND MY FIRST HOME BY TELLING MY SECRETARY THAT I

WAS LOOKING FOR A HOME. SHE TOLD ME OF A CUTE 2 FAMILY HER UNCLE HAD ON THE MARKET. THIS IS THE HOUSE I EVENTUALLY BOUGHT. MAKE A CONCENTRATED EFFORT AND FOCUS ON THAT ONE GOAL. DON'T BE DISTRACTED. JUST KEEP YOUR NOSE TO THE GRINDSTONE UNTIL YOU FIND THE HOME THAT IS MOST APPEALING. THERE IS NO SUCH THING AS THE RIGHT HOUSE, SO DON'T WAIT FOR A FAIRY PRINCESS TO DELIVER ONE. EVEN IF YOU BUILD A HOME FROM THE BASEMENT UP, THERE WILL STILL BE THINGS YOU WOULD HAVE DONE DIFFERENTLY WHEN THE HOME IS COMPLETED.

EVERY FAMILY TODAY NEEDS A HOME. A HOME IS NO LONGER A LUXURY, IT IS A NECESSITY. IT IS ONE OF THE FEW TAX SHELTERS, FORCED SAVING VEHICLES LEFT TO US. DON'T LISTEN TO THOSE WHO WOULD TRY TO TALK YOU OUT OF A HOME PURCHASE. THE LONGER YOU WAIT, THE MORE A HOME WILL COST AND THE HIGHER INTEREST RATES MAY CLIMB. EXPLORE EVERY AVENUE IN YOUR SEARCH, MAGAZINES, NEWSPAPERS, FRIENDS, RELATIVES - YOU MAY EVEN WANT TO RUN YOUR OWN "LOOKING FOR" ADVERTISEMENT.

IF YOU ARE USING A LENDER, THE FINANCIAL TERMS OF THE ARRANGEMENT WILL BE DICTATED BY THEM. BUT IF YOU ARE NEGOTIATING A DEAL WITH AN OWNER ON A PAID OFF PROPERTY, YOU CAN STRIKE ANY DEAL YOU WANT. OBVIOUSLY, IT SHOULD BE BETTER THAN WHAT BANKS ARE OFFERING, SO LOOK FOR THOSE PRIVATE OWNER HELD MORTGAGES AS WELL. TYPICAL LENDER QUALIFYING RATIOS TO DETERMINE MORTGAGE AMOUNT IS GIVEN IN THE FOLLOWING EXAMPLE.

HAVING A GENERAL "FEEL" FOR AREA INTEREST RATES, A BORROWER CAN COMPLETE THE EQUATION, AS SHOWN IN THE FOLLOWING EXAMPLE:

EXAMPLE:
  A. BORROWERS CAN EARN $36,000 GROSS INCOME/YEAR ($3,000 MO.).
  B. BORROWERS ARE INTERESTED IN A SPECIFIC AREA OF THEIR CITY WHERE TAXES GENERALLY RUN $1,800/YR. ($150/MO.).
  C. BORROWER'S ESTIMATE HOMEOWNER'S INSURANCE TO BE $360/YEAR ($30/MO.).
  D. BORROWER WILL HAVE ONE "LONG TERM DEBT" AFTER CLOSING, AMOUNTING TO A $200/MO. PAYMENT).

CALCULATIONS:

A. $3,000/MO.   INCOME X   26 PERCENT = $840.

B. $3,000/MO.   INCOME X   36 PERCENT = $1,080.

C. MONTHLY TAX AND INSURANCE
   PAYMENTS SHOULD BE
   $150 + $30   = $ 180.

ANALYSIS

   A. THIS BORROWER CAN AFFORD $840 - $180 OR $660/MO. IN PRINCIPAL INTEREST PAYMENTS TO MEET RATIO # 1 (28 PERCENT). AVERAGE 30 YR. MORTGAGE RATES ARE 8 PERCENT. $660/MO. AT 8 PERCENT ALLOWS A BORROWER A MORTGAGE AMOUNT OF APPROXIMATELY $90,000
   B. THIS BORROWER CAN AFFORD $1,080 - $380 ($380 REPRESENTS TOTAL OF MONTHLY TAX, INSURANCE, AND DEBT PAYMENTS) OR $700/MO. IN PRINCIPAL AND INTEREST PAYMENTS TO MEET RATIO #2 (36 PERCENT). SINCE BOTH RATIOS MUST BE MET, A BORROWER WITH THE ABOVE CHARACTERISTICS WOULD QUALIFY FOR A $90,000 MORTGAGE. THE BORROWER HAS PREVIOUSLY DETERMINED WHAT CASH INVESTMENT THEY WILL MAKE IN THE NEW HOME. ADDING CASH INVESTMENT TO THE AVAILABLE MORTGAGE AMOUNT GIVES THE PRICE RANGE THAT APPLICANT SHOULD BE SEARCHING IN.

OTHER FACTORS:

DIFFERENT LENDERS MAY DEVIATE SLIGHTLY FROM THE 28%/36% FIGURE USED IN THE ANALYSIS. ALSO, DIFFERENT TYPES OF MORTGAGES MAY USE SLIGHTLY DIFFERENT RATIOS. FOR EXAMPLE, IN AN ADJUSTABLE RATE LOAN WHERE IT IS KNOWN PAYMENTS WILL RISE FROM THE FIRST YEAR AMOUNTS, MORE CONSERVATIVE RATIOS WILL BE APPLIED TO ALLOW FOR FUTURE RATE INCREASES. ALTERNATELY, FHA LOANS ALLOWS SLIGHTLY HIGHER RATIOS.

* *EXAMPLE BORROWED WITH PERMISSION, SYRACUSE SECURITIES MTG. CO.

Alan Ray Hoxie

AUCTIONS

IF YOU ARE THINKING OF SELLING YOUR HOME BY AUCTION, YOU'VE PROBABLY HAD IT ON THE MARKET A WHILE AND ARE LOOKING AT THIS VEHICLE AS A FINAL ALTERNATIVE. CONTRARY TO POPULAR BELIEF, AUCTIONS WON'T DO MORE FOR YOU THAN YOU COULD HAVE DONE HAD YOU BEEN WILLING TO ADJUST YOUR PRICE IN THE FIRST PLACE.

AUCTIONS MAY GENERATE A FEEDING FRENZY OF SORTS, AND THAT IS WHAT AUCTIONEERS RELY ON, BUT THE PEOPLE BIDDING KNOW WHAT COMPARABLE PROPERTIES SELL FOR AND ARE THERE FOR A "DEAL." IF THEY CAN'T GET A "DEAL," THEY DROP OUT. WHEN YOU GO THE AUCTION ROUTE, USUALLY YOU, THE SELLER, HAVE TO PAY FOR ADVERTISING WHICH COULD BE WELL OVER $1.000. YOU WANT HEAVY ADVERTISING TO REACH ALL PROSPECTIVE BUYERS IN A SHORT PERIOD OF TIME, BUT WHAT IF IT RAINS OR SNOWS THE DAY OF THE AUCTION? IF THE AUCTION IS UNRESERVED, THE HIGHEST BID GETS THE PROPERTY, REGARDLESS. IF YOU, THE SELLER, DON'T WANT TO TAKE THAT BID, YOU MUST BID ALSO AND END UP PAYING A TEN

PERCENT BUYERS PREMIUM TO GET YOUR PROPERTY BACK! I HAVE SEEN THIS ON MANY OCCASIONS. MANY PROPERTY AUCTIONEERS DON'T HANDLE RESERVE AUCTIONS WITH A FLOOR ON PRICE BECAUSE THERE IS NO GUARANTEE FOR THEM THAT THEIR TIME WILL BE COMPENSATED. SELLING BY AUCTION, HOWEVER, IS SOMETIMES THE BEST WAY TO DISPOSE OF LARGE PARCELS OF LAND, HOMES THAT NEED MUCH REPAIR, AND HOMES IN A SPARSELY POPULATED COUNTRY SETTING WITHOUT MANY CURRENT COMPARABLE SALES. ALTHOUGH AUCTIONS ARE BECOMING INCREASINGLY POPULAR, I WOULD NOT RECOMMEND THEM FOR YOUR PERSONAL RESIDENCE SINCE I FEEL THAT A GOOD DEAL OF YOUR EQUITY COULD BE SACRIFICED. IT'S PROBABLY O.K. FOR MAMA'S ESTATE IN WISCONSIN THAT YOU AND YOUR FOUR BROTHERS INHERITED OR FOR THE HUNTER'S CAMP UP NORTH.

THE THREE MOST COMMON AUCTIONS YOU WILL SEE ARE TAX AUCTIONS BY A MUNICIPALITY, BANK FORECLOSURE AUCTIONS, AND UNRESERVED ESTATE AUCTIONS. IN BANK AUCTIONS, YOU COULD APPROACH THE BANK ON A CERTAIN PROPERTY, ASK THEM TO QUALIFY YOU FOR A MORTGAGE UP TO AN

AMOUNT BOTH YOU AND THE BANK FEEL YOU CAN HANDLE, AND GO TO THE AUCTION WITH A PRE-APPROVED LIMIT ON A PARTICULAR PROPERTY. IF THE TURNOUT OF BIDDERS IS LARGE, YOU WILL PROBABLY NOT GET A SUPER DEAL. THE MORE WORK THE HOMES NEEDS OR THE MORE MARGINAL THE NEIGHBORHOOD, THE BETTER DEAL YOU ARE LIKELY TO GET. DON'T WAIT UNTIL THE DAY OF THE AUCTION TO PRE-QUALIFY. YOU CAN CALL BANKS OR AUCTIONEERS AND RECEIVE A LIST OF PROPERTIES TO BE AUCTIONED. AGAIN, CALL THE MUNICIPALITY TO FIND OUT WHAT CODE VIOLATIONS EXIST. CHECK FAIR MARKET COMPARABLE SALES IN THE AREA, AND SET YOUR BIDDING LIMIT ACCORDINGLY, INCLUDING A TYPICAL 10% BUYER'S PREMIUM.

TAX AUCTIONS ARE ADVERTISED IN YOUR LOCAL NEWSPAPER AND CONSIST OF PROPERTIES WHICH HAVE BEEN TAX DELINQUENT FOR A PERIOD OF TIME, PERHAPS TWO OR THREE YEARS. THIS IS A GOOD PLACE TO PICK UP A BARGAIN SINCE THE MUNICIPALITY SIMPLY WANTS TO BE RELIEVED OF THESE PROPERTIES AND HAVE THEM BACK ON THE TAX ROLLS. THESE PROPERTIES ARE GENERALLY WITHOUT MORTGAGES SINCE ANY MORTGAGE

HOLDER WOULD MOVE TO PROTECT ITS INTEREST BEFORE THE TAX AUCTION ACTUALLY COULD OCCUR.

SOME PEOPLE DON'T LIKE THE INFERENCE IN AUCTIONS SINCE WE ARE TAKING ADVANTAGE OF ANOTHER PERSON'S MISFORTUNE BY BIDDING ON PROPERTY OF ANOTHER UNFORTUNATE INDIVIDUAL. THAT, MY FRIENDS, IS LIFE. THERE WILL ALWAYS BE DEATH, DIVORCES, BANKRUPTCIES, LOSS OF EMPLOYMENT, ETC. YOU WILL NEVER STOP THESE THINGS FROM HAPPENING, EVEN IN THE BEST OF TIMES, SO WHY NOT TAKE ADVANTAGE OF A GOOD DEAL WHEN YOU CAN. IF YOU THINK THAT YOU DON'T HAVE TO LOOK OUT FOR YOURSELF, TRY COUNTING YOUR FRIENDS IN BANKRUPTCY COURT. IT WON'T TAKE YOU LONG.

AUCTIONS ARE A GOOD WAY TO ACQUIRE PROPERTY FOR LITTLE DOWN AND FOR A GREATLY REDUCED PRICE. ASK THE BANK OR OTHER LENDERS TO LET YOU FINANCE THE ENTIRE AMOUNT, INCLUDING DOWN PAYMENT AND CLOSING COSTS. MANY WILL LET YOU DO THIS ON AN AUCTION PROPERTY. REMEMBER, WHEN INVOLVED IN AUCTION BUYING, KNOW THE AREA, KNOW THE

STATUS OF CODE VIOLATIONS, AND KNOW THE PROPERTY. TAKE A HOME INSPECTOR OR CONTRACTOR THROUGH ONE OR TWO PROPERTIES YOU INTEND TO BID ON. LINE UP YOUR FINANCING AHEAD OF TIME, AND SET A LIMIT ON YOUR BIDDING. WHEN YOU GO TO ATLANTIC CITY TO GAMBLE YOU SET A LIMIT, HOPEFULLY. YOU SHOULD AT AUCTIONS, AS WELL. IT IS EASY TO GET CAUGHT UP IN THE BIDDING FRENZY OF THE MOMENT. THIS IS WHAT AUCTIONEERS RELY ON. AUCTIONEERS ARE GREAT PSYCHOLOGISTS AND KNOW WELL OF THE "GREED FACTOR" IN ALL OF US. DON'T PLAY THEIR GAME, PLAY YOUR GAME. YOU MAY HAVE TO ATTEND SEVERAL AUCTIONS TO FEEL COMFORTABLE BIDDING OR TO FIND THE RIGHT PROPERTY, BUT IF THIS EFFORT SAVES YOU THOUSANDS OF DOLLARS, IT WAS WORTH YOUR EFFORT. I GO TO AUCTIONS JUST TO GET A FEEL FOR THE PRICE OF BOATS OR CARS OR HOMES. THE DEALS I SEE PEOPLE GET ON CARS AND BOATS MAKES ME QUITE SURE I WILL NEVER VISIT A NEW CAR LOT OR NEW BOAT DEALERSHIP AGAIN. YOU WILL BUILD UP YOUR EQUITY POSITION FASTER BY BUYING PROPERTIES THAT NEED WORK THAN BY BUYING NEW AND EXPECTING APPRECIATION ALONE

TO BUILD YOUR NEST EGG. MANY FAMILIES ARE IN A FINANCIAL BIND TODAY BECAUSE THEY BOUGHT A HOME NEEDING BOTH INCOMES TO PAY THE MORTGAGE. WHEN THEIR COMPANY DOWNSIZED AND ONE JOB WAS CUT, WHAT THEN? THIS RECESSION WAS NOT CREATED BY THE JAPANESE OR ANYONE ELSE. IT WAS CREATED BY OUR OWN GREED. WE HAVE HAD TO HAVE A NEW HOUSE THAT ONLY TWO SALARIES COULD AFFORD. WE HAD TO HAVE ALL THE EXTRAS RIGHT AWAY SO WE CHARGED EVERYTHING ON CREDIT CARDS INSTEAD OF SAVING, HOPING THAT TOMORROW WE COULD PAY IT OFF. THIS RECESSION DIDN'T JUST HAPPEN. WE CREATED IT WITH OUR GREED AND OUR CREDIT CARDS. AS A PEOPLE, WE HAVE TERRIBLE SAVINGS HABITS. WE DON'T SAVE, WE SPEND. NOW IT HAS COME HOME TO ROOST. WE NEED TO SLOW DOWN, DOWNSIZE, BECOME LEANER AND MEANER, NOT FATTER AND DEEPER IN DEBT. THE PROBLEM OF GREED EXTENDS TO OUR SAVINGS AND LOANS WHO TOOK A CHANCE ON LENDING TO EXPAND THEIR PORTFOLIOS, TO OUR COMPANIES AND UNIONS TO EXPAND THEIR INFLUENCE, AND OUR GOVERNMENT WHO TRIED TO PROVIDE ALL THINGS TO ALL PEOPLE. WHAT CAUSED

Alan Ray Hoxie

OUR RECESSION IS THAT THE BALLOON BURST FOR EVERYBODY AT THE SAME TIME. WE WILL BE FORCED TO ASSUME CONSERVATIVE SPENDING FOR A WHILE, BUT WE'LL EMERGE FROM THIS A STRONGER, RICHER NATION IN A SHORT TIME.

IN THE MEANTIME, THIS IS A GREAT TIME TO INVEST IN REAL ESTATE AND TECH STOCKS INCLUDING DOT COMS, WHILE VALUES ARE DOWN AND INTEREST RATES ARE, ALSO. REMEMBER, THERE WERE STILL QUITE A FEW MILLIONAIRES DURING THE GREAT DEPRESSION AND THEY GOT RICHER, NOT POORER. A RECESSION IS A SELF-FULFILLING PROPHECY. IF YOU BELIEVE IT'S HERE AND THERE'S NOTHING TO BE DONE ABOUT IT, IT WILL NEVER GO AWAY. IF YOU BELIEVE THAT IT IS NOTHING BUT A SELF-CORRECTING MEASURE, YOU WILL LOOK FOR GOOD DEALS AND WAYS TO PROTECT YOUR INCOME FROM THE NEXT RECESSION. DO YOU LOOK AT THE GLASS AS HALF FULL OR HALF EMPTY? DO SOME RESEARCH, LOOK AT PROPERTIES, TAKE SOME CHANCES AND BID, BID UNTIL YOU GET SOMETHING AT A GOOD PRICE. YOU'LL FEEL BETTER ABOUT CONTROLLING YOUR OWN DESTINY RATHER THAN WAITING AROUND FOR SOMEONE TO HAND YOU A

DEAL. BECOME A PLAYER, NOT A SPECTATOR. THIS TAKES GUTS WHICH MOST PEOPLE DON'T HAVE. THIS IS WHY THOSE NO-MONEY DOWN BOOKS AND TAPES COSTING $300 OR $400 SIT ON THE SHELF AND COLLECT DUST. DON'T LET REAL ESTATE PURCHASING OVERWHELM YOU. GO OUT AND LOOK AND RESEARCH AND LOOK AGAIN, AND ALWAYS KEEP IN MIND THE FACT THAT YOU ARE A BUYER, NOT JUST A LOOKER. DON'T LET ANYTHING OR ANYONE DISSUADE YOU. KEEP TELLING YOURSELF YOU WILL BUY. YOU WILL FIND ENOUGH PEOPLE WHO WILL HELP YOU MAKE YOUR DREAM A REALITY.

Alan Ray Hoxie

GRIEVING YOUR ASSESSMENT (PROPERTY TAXES)

IN ATTEMPTING TO MAKE THIS BOOK AS ALL ENCOMPASSING AS POSSIBLE FOR THE HOMEOWNER, I HAVE DECIDED TO ADD THIS CHAPTER SINCE I REPRESENT HOMEOWNERS IN PROPERTY TAX GRIEVANCES IN MY AREA.

THIS AREA OF PROPERTY TAXATION IS THE LEAST UNIFORM, LEAST REGULATED, AND LEAST UNDERSTOOD OF ALL OF OUR TAXES. FROM THE BEGINNING, WE HAVE PAID TAXES FOR SCHOOL SYSTEMS, FIRE DEPARTMENTS, HIGHWAY SERVICE, ETC., BASED ON A PERCENTAGE OF WHAT SOMEONE BELIEVES OUR PROPERTY IS WORTH. ALL PROPERTY VALUATION BY MUNICIPALITY IS BASED ON ACTUAL CURRENT WORTH. YOU ARE BEING TAXED ON THE ESTIMATED VALUE OF YOUR PROPERTY. WHY DO YOU THINK THAT TOWNS AND CITIES REQUIRE BUILDING PERMITS FOR ADDITIONS, POOLS, ETC. PART OF IT IS TO ENSURE A SAFE STRUCTURE, ESPECIALLY IF THE ADDITION INVOLVES TWO STORIES OR MORE.

AFTER YOUR SKETCH AND PROPOSAL LEAVES THE CODE AND BUILDING PERMIT OFFICE, IT GOES TO THE ASSESSOR WHO FIGURES OUT WHAT ADDITIONAL VALUE THIS ADDS TO YOUR HOME. YOUR ASSESSMENT AND SUBSEQUENT TAXES ARE ADJUSTED ACCORDINGLY. YOUR TAXES MAY GO UP TEMPORARILY IF YOU ARE SUBJECT TO CERTAIN SPECIAL ASSESSMENTS SUCH AS SIDEWALK IMPROVEMENTS, STREET LIGHT IMPROVEMENTS OR SEWER IMPROVEMENTS. THESE CHARGES GO AWAY AFTER THE IMPROVEMENT IS PAID OFF.

THERE ARE A FEW MAJOR REASONS WHY PROPERTY TAXES ARE SO DIVERGENT IN AREAS THAT ARE CLOSELY BOUNDARIED. ONE IS THAT OLDER HOMES HAVE BEEN ASSESSED LONGER AGO AND THAT FORMULA HAS CHANGED OVER THE YEARS TO THE DETRIMENT OF NEWER HOMES NEARBY. IN MY AREA, FOR EXAMPLE, A 60-YEAR OLD HOME I SOLD HAD TOTAL TAXES OF $1,000 AND SOLD FOR $75,000. TWO BLOCKS AWAY, A HOME ONLY 30 YEARS OLD SOLD FOR $65,000.00, BUT HAD TOTAL TAXES OF $2,100. MUNICIPALITIES ARE ACTUALLY AWARE OF THIS DISCREPANCY, BUT HESITATE TO SUGGEST REASSESSMENT BECAUSE OF THE TREMENDOUS

EXPENSE AND POLITICAL FALLOUT. REAL ESTATE APPRAISERS AND PROPERTY EVALUATORS ARE SCARCE AND GOOD ONES ARE RARE. A MUNICIPALITY WOULD RATHER REDUCE THE TAXES OF THOSE WHO HAVE A LEGITIMATE GRIEVANCE THAN PAY FOR A WHOLESALE REEVALUATION OF EVERY PROPERTY, AND, IN MY OPINION, RIGHTLY SO. THOSE WHO WON'T OR DON'T COMPLAIN ABOUT THEIR TAXES, LET THEM BE. WHO CARES IF THEY DON'T CARE? BUT THOSE WHO CAN SHOW LEGITIMATE INEQUALITY WILL BE GIVEN RELIEF. WHY? BECAUSE THEY CAN SHOW INEQUALITY AND THEY HAVE TAKEN THE TIME TO GRIEVE THEIR SITUATION. WHAT IS INVOLVED IN GRIEVING YOUR ASSESSMENT OR TAXES? IT'S NOT THAT HARD.

ANYONE CAN DO IT. WETHER YOU BOUGHT YOUR HOME RECENTLY DOES NOT MATTER. GET A WRITTEN MARKET ANALYSIS FROM TWO OR THREE REAL ESTATE AGENTS. ALSO, ASK FOR RECENT SALES OF SIMILAR PROPERTIES IN YOUR AREA. LOOK AT THE TOTAL TAX FIGURE ON THESE RECENT SALES. THIS IS YOUR AMMUNITION. IF THE TOTAL TAXES ON SIMILARLY VALUED PROPERTY IS LESS, YOU'VE GOT A GREAT CASE. IF NOT, YOU DON'T. ALL THIS TAKES

VERY LITTLE TIME. YOU CAN ALSO GO TO YOUR ASSESSOR'S OFFICE AND RESEARCH YOUR NEIGHBOR'S TAXES OR TAXES ON RECENT, SIMILAR SALES IN YOUR AREA. THIS IS PUBLIC INFORMATION.

REMEMBER, YOU HAVE TO MAKE THE CASE FOR REDUCTION, NOT THE MUNICIPALITY. THE BURDEN OF PROOF IS ON YOU. THE STRONGER YOUR CASE, THE BETTER YOUR CHANCE OF A REDUCTION. AS MENTIONED IN THE EARLIER CHAPTER ON SETTING A SELLING PRICE, HIRE A CERTIFIED OR LICENSED APPRAISER AND ASK FOR A TWO PAGE NARRATIVE. USUALLY, YOU'LL GET ONE FOR UNDER $150. IF YOU SAVE $500 IN TAXES YOUR FIRST YEAR, IT'S A DEAL. REMEMBER, IF SUCCESSFUL, YOU NOT ONLY SAVE THE FIRST YEAR BUT IN ALL SUBSEQUENT YEARS BECAUSE YOUR BASIS IS REDUCED. I HAVE DONE THIS ON TWO OF MY INCOME PROPERTIES TWICE IN FOUR YEARS AND WON BOTH TIMES ON BOTH HOMES.

ASSESSMENT REVIEW BOARDS ARE GENERALLY MADE UP OF REGULAR CITIZENS APPOINTED BY TOWN BOARDS OR CITY COUNCILS AND HAVE THE POWER TO REDUCE RESIDENTIAL PROPERTY TAXES. THERE IS USUALLY SOMEONE ON THAT BOARD WHO HAS EXPERIENCE AS AN APPRAISER OR BROKER, OR

Alan Ray Hoxie

THERE IS ASSISTANCE FROM LEGAL COUNSEL. THE DEPARTMENT OF ASSESSMENT PRESENTS THE CITY OR TOWN'S CASE AND YOU PRESENT YOURS, ALL THEY WANT TO HEAR IS THE FACTS. SO PRESENT THE FACTS. YOUR APPRAISAL OR PURCHASE PRICE IS $95,000. SHOW THEM HOW HOMES COMPARABLE IN YOUR AREA THAT HAVE SOLD FOR $95,000 ALL HAVE TAX SITUATIONS OF $500 TO $1,000.00 LESS THAN YOURS AND SIMPLY ASK FOR EQUALITY. DON'T RANT AND RAVE ABOUT THE CONSTITUTION AND ABOUT TAXES AND THE GOVERNMENT, ETC. YOU ARE TALKING TO SYMPATHETIC, APPOINTED (FOR A VERY NOMINAL SALARY) PUBLIC SERVANTS WHO WANT TO SHOW THAT THEY HAVE MADE SOME REDUCTIONS. GIVE THEM REASON FOR YOU TO BE ONE. THIS ARENA IS ONE OF THE LEAST ADVERSARIAL I HAVE EVER BEEN IN. BRING THREE COMPARABLE PROPERTIES RECENTLY SOLD WITH LESSER TAXES THAN YOURS AND YOU SHOULD BE GOLDEN, MORE IF YOU CAN FIND THEM. GIVE THEM WHAT THEY WANT. IF THEY WANT A SUGGESTED ASSESSMENT FIGURE, INSTEAD OF A TAX AMOUNT, GIVE THAT. THIS IS USUALLY ON A PRINTOUT. THE ASSESSED VALUE WILL HAVE A CORRELATION TO TOTAL TAXES. IT

WILL BE EASY TO SEE WHEN YOU COMPARE THE THREE RECENTLY SOLD PROPERTIES TO YOURS.

IF YOUR PROPERTY WARRANTS THIS TYPE OF ACTION, IT IS DEFINITELY WORTH IT NOW IN TERMS OF IMMEDIATE SAVINGS AND IN THE FUTURE IN TERMS OF MARKETABILITY. REMEMBER, WHETHER A REAL ESTATE AGENT GETS THIS INFORMATION FOR YOU OR YOU GO TO THE ASSESSOR, THIS INFORMATION IS A MATTER OF PUBLIC RECORD AND IS IN NO WAY SECRET AS MANY PEOPLE BELIEVE. REMEMBER TO COMPARE APPLES TO APPLES. DON'T COMPARE THE HOME ACROSS THE STREET WITH THREE STORIES, THREE CAR GARAGE, POOL, JACUZZI, TENNIS COURTS, TO YOUR TWO BEDROOM RANCH, UNLESS YOU BUILT IT ON AN OIL WELL. BE POLITE AND STAY FOCUSED. AND STICK TO THE FACTS. JUST STICK TO THE FACTS, MA'AM.

Alan Ray Hoxie

NEGOTIATING - GETTING YOUR THOUGHTS ACROSS

AS I MENTIONED IN AN EARLIER CHAPTER, HE WHO HAS POSSESSION OF PROPERTY HAS THE HAMMER. AS A SELLER, YOU KNOW WHAT YOUR BOTTOM LINE IS AND WILL PROBABLY NOT BE THE FIRST TO SUGGEST CREATIVE FINANCING. AFTER ALL, YOU WANT I 00% CASH AT CLOSING, RIGHT? YOU DON'T WANT TO SUGGEST ANY CREATIVE FINANCING EXCEPT AS PART OF A NEGOTIATION STANCE BROUGHT UP BY A BUYER. AS THE SELLER, THERE ARE MANY DIFFERENT ARRANGEMENTS YOU COULD LIVE WITH, INCLUDING ALL CASH AT CLOSING. HOWEVER, FOR TAX PURPOSES, THERE ARE SEVERAL OTHER ATTRACTIVE ALTERNATIVES. IT IS UP TO THE BUYER, HOWEVER, TO SUGGEST THEM. AS A BUYER, YOU PROBABLY HAVE MUCH TO OFFER, MANY DREAMS, ASPIRATIONS, MAYBE A JOB, A REPUTATION FOR HARD WORK AND HONESTY, BUT IF YOU'RE LIKE MOST AMERICANS, YOU DON'T HAVE MUCH MONEY TO SPARE FOR A DOWN PAYMENT FOR ANY PROPERTY, ESPECIALLY INVESTMENT PROPERTY. LENDERS TODAY ARE BECOMING MORE AND MORE

CONSERVATIVE AND NOW DEMAND BETWEEN 25% AND 30% DOWN ON INVESTMENT PROPERTY. MANY LENDERS HAVE GIVEN UP THIS TYPE OF LENDING ALTOGETHER BECAUSE OF THE RISK. THIS IS WHY PRIVATE MORTGAGES WILL BECOME EVER MORE POPULAR IN THE '90's. HOWEVER, THIS MAKES IT MORE IMPORTANT FOR YOU, THE BUYER, TO BE ABLE TO EFFECTIVELY NEGOTIATE WITH SELLERS TO ACQUIRE THE PROPERTIES YOU WANT. YOU WON'T BE DEALING WITH A WHITE COLLAR EXECUTIVE SITTING AT A DESK IN SOME LARGE BANK. YOU'LL BE DEALING WITH FARMERS, RETIRED POSTMEN , FIREMEN, COPS, IMMIGRANT LANDOWNERS, PEOPLE OF ALL RACES AND ETHNIC BACKGROUNDS. NO AMOUNT OF REAL ESTATE KNOWLEDGE GAINED FROM BOOKS AND TAPES IS GOING TO MAKE YOU ANY BETTER AT DEALING WITH PEOPLE. AND IF YOU CAN'T EFFECTIVELY DEAL WITH OTHERS TO GET THEM TO RESPECT YOU AND WANT TO HELP YOU, YOU WON'T HAVE TO WORRY ABOUT THE TOUGH PART, TENANTS, BECAUSE YOU WON'T HAVE ANY PROPERTY TO MANAGE. I LISTEN TO TAPES AND READ BOOKS, NOT SO MUCH ON REAL ESTATE BUT ON THE

ART OF NEGOTIATING AND HOW BEST TO COMMUNICATE AND DEAL WITH OTHERS.

WHEN YOU ARE TRYING TO GET A PROPERTY THAT IS WORTH ANYTHING FROM THE OWNER FOR VERY LITTLE MONEY DOWN, YOU'D BETTER DO A LOT OF FAST TALKING. THAT'S WHAT IT WILL TAKE. THE LESS MONEY DOWN, THE BETTER NEGOTIATOR YOU'LL HAVE TO BE.

LANDLORDS HAVE HEARD ALL THE CLICHES FROM THE REAL ESTATE TAPES AND IT DIDN'T WORK FOR MANY OTHER FOLKS AND IT'S NOT GOING TO WORK FOR YOU. YOU'VE GOT TO CONVINCE A SELLER, IN YOUR OWN WORDS, OF THE BENEFITS NOT ONLY OF SELLING FOR VERY LITTLE DOWN, BUT OF SELLING TO YOU. WHY SHOULD THIS SELLER TRUST YOU? WHAT IS YOUR BACKGROUND; WHAT GUARANTEES WILL HE HAVE? HE HAS MORE AT STAKE THAN EVEN YOUR EMPLOYER. YOUR BOSS CAN ALWAYS FIRE YOU AND YOU'LL BE GONE BEFORE SUNSET. IF YOUR DEAL GOES SOUR WITH A SELLER HOLDING A MORTGAGE, THIS PERSON HAS TO DEAL WITH YOU DURING USUALLY UGLY FORECLOSURE PROCEEDINGS AND THEN CHASE YOU FOR THE MONEY YOU WILL SURELY OWE HIM.

BUYING PROPERTY FROM A PRIVATE MORTGAGE HOLDER IS EVERY BIT LIKE A MARRIAGE. JUST AS YOU WOULD SWEET TALK YOUR DATE TO TRY TO GET WHAT YOU WANT, SO TOO WILL YOU HAVE TO DO THIS WHEN ATTEMPTING TO BUY PROPERTY. YOU CAN CALL THIS KISSING UP, OR SALESMANSHIP, OR ANYTHING YOU WANT. WHAT DO YOU CARE WHAT IT'S CALLED AS LONG AS YOU GET WHAT YOU WANT AND IT PUTS MONEY IN YOUR POCKET AND EVERYONE IS HAPPY IN THE END. TAVERNS ARE FULL OF PEOPLE WHO WON'T COMPROMISE. MOST OF THEM DON'T HAVE ANY MONEY EITHER. WE HAVE TO SELL OURSELVES EVERY DAY IN VARIOUS STAGES OF CONSCIOUSNESS TO GET WHAT WE WANT. OUR PERSUASIVE EFFORTS ARE FAIRLY CONSCIOUS WHEN DEALING WITH OUR CHILDREN TO GET THEM TO CLEAN THEIR ROOMS. HOWEVER, OUR EFFORTS TO CONVINCE AN EMPLOYER TO HIRE US OR A POLICE OFFICER TO FOREGO THAT TICKET ARE MOST COMPLEX AND A MORE SUBCONSCIOUS EFFORT.

LOOK AT THE SELLER AS A PROSPECTIVE EMPLOYER. THE PROPERTY YOU DESIRE WILL PROVIDE MANY TAX BENEFITS IN ADDITION TO A POSITIVE CASH FLOW. THIS OWNER CAN HAVE A

DIRECT INFLUENCE ON YOUR REAL ESTATE PORTFOLIO. IN A WAY, YOU ARE ON A .JOB INTERVIEW WHEN YOU DEAL WITH THAT SELLER.

SELL YOURSELF, YOUR STRONG POINTS, EMPHASIZE YOUR WORK ETHIC. THE BIGGEST FEAR OF SOMEONE WHO CARRIES A MORTGAGE IS THE FEAR OF HAVING TO TAKE THE PROPERTY BACK. ADDRESS THAT FEAR, AND ASSURE THEM THAT IT WON'T HAPPEN. YOU KNOW THEIR ATTORNEY IS GOING TO ADVISE THEM NOT TO HOLD A MORTGAGE FOR UNDER TEN PERCENT DOWN. YOU DON'T HAVE THAT AND WANT THEM TO DO OTHERWISE. THIS WILL TAKE QUICKLY ESTABLISHING TRUST. PEOPLE TRUST ON FEELING AND ON INTUITION IN THE SHORT TERM.

THE METHOD THAT I LIKE TO USE, I THINK, NEEDS FURTHER CLARIFICATION. LET'S SAY YOU SEE A TWO-FAMILY PROPERTY ON THE MARKET FOR $64,000. THE OWNER HAPPENS TO OWN IT FREE AND CLEAR. THERE ARE MANY PROPERTIES OF THIS TYPE. YOU OFFER HIM $50,000 AND GIVE HIM $1,000 OR $2,000 THAT YOU HAVE SAVED OR BORROWED. YOU MAKE AN AGREEMENT WITH HIM TO PAY HIM $400 PER MONTH FOR TWO YEARS. AT THE END OF TWO

YEARS, YOU WILL PUT A BANK MORTGAGE ON THE PROPERTY. THIS IS CALLED A BALLOON MORTGAGE. AT THAT TIME, HE WILL GET THE BALANCE IN FULL. YOU WILL TAKE CARE OF TAXES AND INSURANCE. AT $50,000, YOU HAVE GIVEN HIM $2,000 AT CLOSING, EQUALS $52,000. AT $400 PER MONTH, WHICH YOU COLLECT FROM THE TENANTS , HOPEFULLY YOU COLLECT TWICE THAT MUCH PER MONTH, OVER TWO YEARS THAT AMOUNTS TO $9,600. WHEN YOU ADD THAT TO $52,000.00, HE HAS $61,600 OR ONLY $2,400 LESS THAN A FULL PRICE OFFER, PLUS NO COMMISSION.

IN THIS WAY, YOU AVOID THE 25% OR 30% DOWN REQUIRED BY LENDERS BECAUSE YOU ALREADY OWN THE PROPERTY WHEN YOU GO TO THE BANK FOR A MORTGAGE. TO PAY THE GUY AT THE END OF TWO YEARS, THE TRANSACTION BECOMES SIMPLY A REFINANCE AND NOT A PURCHASE. BANKS ARE MORE WILLING TO DO THIS.

IN THIS "WIN-WIN" SITUATION, YOU GET YOUR PROPERTY AND ESTABLISHED CASH FLOW. HE GETS HIS MONEY MONTHLY OVER A SHORT TERM AND GETS OUT COMPLETELY IN ONLY TWO YEARS. EVERYONE IS HAPPY. IN THE MEANTIME, DURING THE

TWO-YEAR PERIOD, YOU RAISE YOUR RENTS TO WHATEVER IS MARKET OR TO THE TOP OF WHAT IS BEING PAID IN THE AREA. YOU DO THIS SO THAT THE BANK WILL MORTGAGE THE WHOLE AMOUNT OF THE PAYOFF, SOMETHING VERY COMMONLY DONE. TO PAY OFF THE $50,000 OWNER-HELD MORTGAGE, THE HOUSE ONLY HAS TO APPRAISE FOR $67,000. IN ALMOST ALL CASES, THIS WOULD BE NO PROBLEM SINCE NEIGHBORHOODS USUALLY DON'T CHANGE RADICALLY IN TWO YEARS. THIS IS ON A 75% LOAN TO VALUE RATIO WHICH IS THE LOWEST RATIO I'VE SEEN BANKS USE IN INVESTOR OWNED PROPERTY. MANY BANKS WILL USE AN 80% RATIO, WHICH IS BETTER FOR YOU. THE HIGHER THE RENTS ARE, THE MORE THE PROPERTY WILL APPRAISE FOR. THIS IS ALMOST ALWAYS THE CASE IN INCOME PRODUCING PROPERTY.

IN ATTEMPTING TO PURCHASE PROPERTIES, YOU WILL BE USING ONLY "WIN-WIN" TECHNIQUES. YOU GET WHAT YOU WANT AND THE SELLER GETS WHAT HE WANTS. NO ONE IS BEING BULLIED OR PRESSURED INTO ANYTHING. FIND OUT FIRST THE REASON THE OWNER WANTS TO SELL. IF HE'S OUT OF TOWN MOST OF THE YEAR AND RETIRED, HE WANTS A MONTHLY

CASH FLOW AND NO HEADACHES. YOU WILL TAKE CARE OF THAT.

SECONDLY, CALL THE CITY OR TOWN CODES DEPARTMENT AND FIND OUT IF THE PROPERTY IS OR IS NOT IN VIOLATION OF CODE AND TO WHAT EXTENT. THIS IS PUBLIC INFORMATION THAT CAN BE REQUESTED BY ANYONE. IS THERE A MORTGAGE? IF NOT, GOOD. IF SO, IS IT ASSUMABLE? DO NOT ACT TOO INTERESTED IN THE PROPERTY. AS WE SAID EARLIER, "YOU CAN'T MARRY EVERY GIRL YOU DANCE WITH. " ACT AS IF YOU COULD CARE LESS WHETHER YOU GET THE PROPERTY OR NOT AND WHAT A HEADACHE IT WILL BE, BUT TO HELP YOU OUT, MR. SELLER, HERE IS WHAT I'M WILLING TO DO. DIFFERENT PEOPLE HAVE TO BE APPROACHED DIFFERENTLY. FIND OUT THEIR CONCERNS AND ADDRESS THEM.

BUY YOURSELF AN AMORTIZATION BOOK AT ANY BOOK STORE. THIS WILL TELL YOU THE PRINCIPLE AND INTEREST PAYMENT OF A SPECIFIC AMOUNT OF MONEY AT A GIVEN PERCENTAGE RATE OVER A PERIOD OF YEARS. TO THAT YOU CAN ADD A MONTHLY PROPERTY TAX AMOUNT AND INSURANCE. YOU THEN SUBTRACT THAT FROM YOUR RENTS TO

FIGURE OUT YOUR CASH FLOW AND HOW MUCH TO OFFER AN OWNER FOR THE PROPERTY. LET'S ASSUME YOU'RE NOT GOING TO PUT DOWN MORE THAN 2,000 IN ANY CASE. IF AN OWNER WANTS $80,000 FOR HIS TWO FAMILY AND HIS RENTS ARE $325 AND $325 PER MONTH, THERE IS NO WAY YOU CAN BUY THAT PROPERTY FOR EVEN CLOSE TO WHAT HE WANTS SINCE THE RENTS WON'T COVER YOUR MONTHLY PAYMENT TO HIM, PLUS TAXES AND OTHER COSTS. HE HAS HURT HIMSELF BY KEEPING HIS RENTS TOO LOW FOR THAT VALUABLE A PIECE OF PROPERTY. IF YOU ARE UNSURE ABOUT WHAT RENTS COULD BE IN THE AREA, CALL SOME OWNERS AND ASK THEM WHAT THEY CHARGE OR CALL LOCAL REAL ESTATE AGENTS TO ASK THE SAME QUESTION. WHEN YOU LOCATE A PROPERTY THAT YOU ARE INTERESTED IN OBTAINING, CALL ANY REAL ESTATE OFFICE AND ASK THEM WHAT COMPARABLE PROPERTIES ARE SELLING FOR IN THAT AREA AND WHAT RENTS ARE. MANY TIMES THE RENTS ARE LISTED IN THE PRINTOUTS OF CLOSED PROPERTIES. THIS WILL GIVE YOU A RANGE OF VALUE TO MAKE A SAFE OFFER ON THE HOUSE. REMEMBER TO STAY BELOW MARKET VALUE SINCE THERE IS NO REAL ESTATE

COMMISSION INVOLVED, ASSUMING YOU ARE DOING THIS ON YOUR OWN. IF THE HOME IS IN THE HANDS OF REAL ESTATE, OFFER TO PAY THE COMMISSION INSTEAD OF A DOWN PAYMENT. PERHAPS EVEN TO PAY PART OF THE COMMISSION OVER TIME, OUT OF COLLECTED RENTS. I HAVE HAD EVERYTHING FROM SNOW BLOWERS TO MOTORCYCLES OFFERED TO ME AS PART OF MY COMMISSION. SOME I TAKE, SOME I DON'T. DEVELOP YOUR OWN PLAN OF ACTION.

HOW MUCH CAN YOU PUT DOWN FOR EACH PROPERTY? WHAT PRICE RANGE DO YOU WANT TO STAY IN? HOW MUCH CASH FLOW PER MONTH DO YOU NEED? TRY TO KEEP TO A MINIMUM OF $100 PER MONTH PER UNIT POSITIVE CASH FLOW.

CALL BANKS IN YOUR AREA AND ASK THEM IF THEY WILL MORTGAGE A PROPERTY YOU ALREADY OWN THAT HAS A TWO-YEAR BALLOON MORTGAGE. DON'T WAIT UNTIL THE TWENTY-THIRD MONTH TO START CALLING BANKS. THE GOAL HERE IS TO GET AROUND THE BANKS' 25-30% DOWN REQUIREMENT ON A STRAIGHT PURCHASE. CALL AN ACCOUNTANT OR TAX LAWYER WHO DEALS WITH INVESTMENT PROPERTY, SIMPLY TO INTRODUCE YOURSELF AND ASK FOR THEIR HELP DOWN THE ROAD.

CONTINGENCIES

MANY BUYERS DON'T UNDERSTAND WHAT MAKING AN OFFER WITH A CONTINGENCY REALLY MEANS. A CONTINGENCY IS ANY ITEM INSERTED IN A CONTRACT THAT QUALIFIES THE CONTRACT AND BASICALLY SAYS THAT UNTIL THIS CONTINGENCY IS SATISFIED AND REMOVED, WE REALLY DON'T HAVE AN OFFER EVEN THOUGH EVERYTHING ELSE HAS BEEN AGREED UPON. FOR EXAMPLE, A COMMON CONTINGENCY IS UPON A SATISFACTORY HOME INSPECTION WITHIN FIVE DAYS. THIS MEANS THAT THE BUYER HAS FIVE DAYS TO OBTAIN A SATISFACTORY HOME INSPECTION, USUALLY AT THE BUYERS EXPENSE, AND THEN REMOVE THAT CONTINGENCY TO CONTINUE THE PROGRESS OF THE DEAL. IF YOU HAVE A HOUSE TO SELL AND YOU PUT AN OFFER ON A PROPERTY THAT IS CONTINGENT ON THE SALE OF YOUR HOME, THIS MEANS THAT, ASSUMING ALL OTHER DETAILS ARE ACCEPTABLE, YOU WILL HAVE A DEAL WHEN YOU ACCEPT AN OFFER ON <u>YOUR</u> HOME AND <u>REMOVE</u> THE CONTINGENCY ON THE HOME YOU ARE BUYING. IF, HOWEVER, AN OFFER COMES IN FROM ANOTHER

AGENT ON THE HOME YOU ARE BUYING AND THE SELLERS WANTS TO ACCEPT IT, YOU ARE THEN NOTIFIED AND GIVEN 24 TO 48 HOURS TO REMOVE THE CONTINGENCY OR LOSE THAT HOME. HAVING A CONTINGENCY IS A WEAKER NEGOTIATING POSITION THAN HAVING YOUR HOME ALREADY SOLD. THIS IS WHY IT IS BENEFICIAL TO MARKET YOUR HOME <u>BEFORE</u> YOU BEGIN TO LOOK FOR ANOTHER HOME. YOU CAN ALWAYS ASK YOUR BUYER TO GIVE YOU 30 DAYS TO FIND SUITABLE HOUSING OR YOUR DEAL COULD BE CANCELED. I FEEL THAT HAVING YOUR HOME SOLD AND CONCENTRATING ON FINDING HOUSING IN 30 DAYS IS VERY EASY TO DO. THIS WAY, YOU KNOW MORE WHAT YOU HAVE IN HAND FINANCIALLY. YOU ARE IN A MUCH STRONGER NEGOTIATING POSITION THIS WAY AND MOST LIKELY WILL GET A BETTER DEAL.

THE LONG AND SHORT OF THIS CHAPTER IS SIMPLY TO ASK, ASK, ASK. ASK FOR AS MUCH INFORMATION AS YOU CAN TO MAKE AN INFORMED DECISION. WHERE PEOPLE GET INTO TROUBLE IS WHEN THEY ASSUME TOO MUCH. MY ACCOUNTANT ASSUMED THAT THE RESIDENTIAL UNIT HE WAS BUYING FOR AN OFFICE WAS ZONED FOR THAT SINCE

IT ONCE WAS A GROCERY STORE. HOWEVER, WHEN THE STORE CLOSED, IT REVERTED BACK TO RESIDENTIAL AND HE HAD TO GET A VARIANCE TO OPEN HIS TAX OFFICE. HE NEVER ASKED ABOUT IT. A SIMPLE PHONE CALL TO THE CITY ZONING OFFICE WOULD HAVE REVEALED THAT. HE MAY HAVE BEEN ABLE TO EITHER GET A LOWER PRICE FROM THE SELLER OR OTHER CONCESSIONS BECAUSE OF THIS PROBLEM.

FINALLY, FIND A GOOD HANDYMAN WHO WILL MOW LAWNS, DO SOME LIGHT PLUMBING AND SMALL REPAIRS. I DON'T HAVE A DAY TO SPEND PUTTERING ON A WATER HEATER. KEEP GOOD RECORDS OF WHAT YOU SPEND AND KEEP THEM FOR AT LEAST FIVE YEARS IN CASE OF AN AUDIT.

I HAVE FOUND WHEN WORKING WITH FIRST TIME HOME BUYERS THAT WHEN NEGOTIATING FOR A PROPERTY, IT IS APPROPRIATE TO KEEP IN MIND THAT A PROPERTY IS PRICED SUCH THAT THE SELLER EXPECTS A CUSHION. I AM WORKING WITH A COUPLE WHO SAY THEY HAVE BEEN LOOKING FOR A HOME FOR TWO YEARS. I CAN BELIEVE IT WHEN WE TALK ABOUT OFFERS FOR PROPERTIES THEY ARE INTERESTED IN PURCHASING. THEY SAW A HOME ON

THE MARKET FOR $70,000; THEIR OFFER WAS FOR $58,000 AND, OF COURSE, IT WAS REJECTED AND COUNTERED AT $68,500. AS I EXPLAINED TO THEM, A SELLER WHO MIGHT HAVE ACCEPTED $58,000 WOULD PROBABLY HAVE HIS HOME ON THE MARKET AT $61,000 OR $62,000 AND IF THIS TYPE OF "LOWBALLING" WAS THEIR PREFERRED COURSE OF ACTION, THEY SHOULD CONFINE THEMSELVES TO SEARCHING THAT RANGE AND NOT LOOK AT HOMES PRICED HIGHER THAN $62,000. THEY FELT, HOWEVER, THAT SOMEWHERE THERE EXISTS SOMEONE WHO WILL SAY YES TO ONE OF THEIR MAJOR LEAGUE "LOWBALL" OFFERS. THEY HAVE BEEN LOOKING FOR TWO YEARS AND WILL PROBABLY STILL BE IN THE MARKET TWO YEARS FROM NOW PLAYING THESE TYPES OF GAMES.

AS I SAID IN EARLIER CHAPTERS, THE SELLER ALWAYS HAS THE HAMMER SINCE HE OWNS AND CONTROLS THE PROPERTY. IF YOU, THE BUYER, WANT IT, YOU'RE GOING TO HAVE TO PAY THE PRICE OR NEAR THE PRICE, OR OFFER SOME OTHER COMPENSATING INCENTIVE. TO NEGOTIATE BY SIMPLY RUNNING AROUND TOWN MAKING "LOW BALL" OFFERS, ESPECIALLY ON PROPERTY IN GOOD

SHAPE, IS A WASTE OF EVERYONES TIME. THE BETTER THE CONDITION OF THE SUBJECT PROPERTY, THE CLOSER TO ASKING PRICE YOU WILL HAVE TO PAY FOR IT.

I EXPLAINED TO THIS COUPLE THAT I WAS TRYING TO HELP THEM FIND A HOUSE AND THAT (I DIDN'T CARE IF THEY THREW THEIR MONEY AWAY ON RENT FOR ANOTHER TWO YEARS. THIS WAS NOT GOING TO BOTHER ME SINCE I ALREADY HAVE A HOUSE AND ALL THAT GOES WITH IT. THEY RESPONDED BY ASSURING ME THAT, BY SOME MAGICAL HAPPENING, THEY WERE GOING TO GET THEIR HOME EVEN THOUGH THEY CONSISTENTLY "LOWBALLED" OFFERS BY 20%. IN MY OPINION, IF YOU LIKE A HOME ENOUGH AND IT FITS YOUR NEEDS, MAKE THE HARD DECISION TO BITE THE BULLET. BUY THE HOME SO THAT YOU CAN GO ON TO OTHER THINGS IN YOUR LIFE AND BEGIN BUILDING UP EQUITY. TO ARGUE OVER $2,000 OR $3,000 IN PRICE OVER A 30-YEAR MORTGAGE MAKES NO SENSE TO ME. AT A TEN PERCENT INTEREST RATE, THAT DIFFERENCE WOULD ONLY ADD $5 OR $6 PER MONTH TO YOUR MORTGAGE. THE BOTTOM LINE IS, DO YOU WANT THE HOME THAT YOU LIKED ENOUGH TO PUT AN OFFER ON FOR

ADDITIONAL PENNIES A MONTH? IF SO, STOP STANDING ON PRINCIPLE AND MEET THE SELLER'S OFFER AND BE DONE WITH IT. THEN NEXT TIME YOU GO TO SELL, YOU WILL BE IN A DIFFERENT POWER POSITION AND YOU'LL UNDERSTAND HOW VALUABLE THAT HOME IS TO YOU. FIRST TIME HOME BUYERS DON'T QUITE UNDERSTAND THIS THEORY OF HOME VALUE SINCE THEY DON'T OWN REAL ESTATE AND ARE USUALLY MORE IGNORANT OF THE REAL ESTATE MARKET THAN ANY OTHER BUYING GROUP. THEY MAKE THE UNFORTUNATE MISTAKE OF LISTENING TOO DEEPLY TO DADDY WHO TELLS THEM THAT, 30 YEARS AGO, HE BOUGHT HIS FIRST HOME FOR $10,000 AND THEY CAN GET THE SAME KIND OF DEAL TODAY. AIN'T GONNA HAPPEN!

A SAYING THAT I LIKE IS THAT "LIFE IS HARD BY THE YARD, BUT A CINCH BY THE INCH. " THIS IS NO MORE TRUE THAN IN REAL ESTATE. TACKLE EACH PROPERTY ONE AT A TIME AND EACH PROBLEM ONE AT A TIME. THE PROBLEM WITH THE TAPES ORDERED OVER THE T.V. IS THAT THE AVERAGE PERSON BECOMES OVERWHELMED AT THE VOLUME OF MATERIAL TO DIGEST AND PANIC SETS IN. THESE THINGS THEN COLLECT DUST FOR YEARS WHILE THE

AUTHORS LAUGH ALL THE WAY TO THE BANK. PUT THAT CREDIT CARD AWAY, FOCUS ON ONE HOME AT A TIME AND TAKE THE NECESSARY BABY STEPS TOWARD SELF-RELIANCE. IF THE FIRST PROPERTY YOU BUY IS A 6-UNIT APARTMENT HOUSE, YOU MAY BE IN FOR A BIG SURPRISE AND A FINANCIAL NIGHTMARE. REMEMBER WHEN YOU BUY PROPERTY, YOU NOT ONLY SIGN A MORTGAGE WHICH PLEDGES THE PROPERTY AS COLLATERAL FOR A LOAN, BUT YOU SIGN A PERSONAL PROMISE TO PAY. IF YOU BECOME OVERWHELMED BY BUYING TOO BIG A PROPERTY TOO SOON AND HAVE TO WALK AWAY FROM IT OR THE BANK TAKES IT TO AUCTION, YOU MAY BE RESPONSIBLE FOR THE BALANCE OF THE EXISTING MORTGAGE, MINUS SALE PRICE. DON'T THINK FOR A MINUTE THAT TENANTS AND/OR CITY CODE INSPECTORS ARE EASY TO DEAL WITH BECAUSE THEY ARE NOT. IT WILL TAKE YOU AT LEAST FIVE YEARS TO UNDERSTAND THE IN'S AND OUT'S OF INVESTMENT PROPERTY OWNERSHIP AND ONLY THEN, WHEN YOU ARE ACTIVELY INVOLVED IN THE MANAGEMENT OF THE PROPERTY. YOU WILL WANT TO INVESTIGATE ALL TENANT SUBSIDY PROGRAMS IN YOUR AREA, AND HOW THEY WORK.

THIS, IN ADDITION TO YOUR DAY JOB, IN ADDITION TO CARING FOR YOUR FAMILY, IN ADDITION TO WHATEVER OUTSIDE INTERESTS YOU HAVE. IF A FURNACE GOES IN THE MIDDLE OF WINTER AND YOU HAD MONEY SAVED FOR DISNEY WORLD, BYE BYE DISNEY WORLD. SOME THINGS CAN'T WAIT. LET A PROPERTY GO BY THE BOARDS IF YOU CAN'T NEGOTIATE A DEAL YOU CAN LIVE WITH. EVEN THOUGH YOU ARE ONLY PUTTING A SMALL AMOUNT DOWN, YOUR CREDIT WILL BE HURT IF THE OWNER HAS TO TAKE BACK A PROPERTY. SURE, THERE MAY BE SETBACKS, UNEXPECTED BREAKDOWNS, BUT REAL ESTATE INVESTING SHOULD BE FOR THE LONG TERM, JUST IN CASE. TRY TO PURCHASE THE HOME FOR THE RIGHT PRICE SO THAT IF YOU CANNOT SELL IT FAST ENOUGH, THE RENT COLLECTED WILL COVER ALL EXPENSES AND STILL NET YOU A POSITIVE CASH FLOW. MAKE THAT YOUR BOTTOM LINE WHEN NEGOTIATING AND DON'T DEVIATE FROM IT. KNOWING THE PRICE TO COME IN WITH IS AS IMPORTANT AS THE TERMS.

YOU MAY WANT TO OBTAIN A REAL ESTATE SALES LICENSE AND AFFILIATE WITH A FIRM TO HAVE USE OF THE M.L.S. SYSTEM AND INFORMATION

ON COMPARABLE PROPERTIES. THERE ARE MANY COMPANIES WHO WELCOME PART TIMERS. BECOMING AN INTELLIGENT INVESTOR IN REAL ESTATE IS SIMILAR TO THAT IN ANY OTHER INVESTMENT ARENA. IT TAKES TIME AND STUDY NOT TO GET BURNT. MY FATHER ONCE PUT $30,000 IN STOCK OPTIONS HOPING TO GET RICH QUICK. HE HAD NO KNOWLEDGE OF THE MARKET AND HADN'T FOLLOWED IT TO ANY DEGREE. HE LOST ALL OF IT IN A SHORT PERIOD OF TIME AND MY MOTHER NEVER LETS HIM FORGET IT! THAT SAME MONEY, INVESTED IN REAL ESTATE, WOULD, I'M CERTAIN, HAVE DONE HIM A BETTER DEAL. BUT REAL ESTATE INVESTING SHOULD BE PLANNED FOR THE LONG HAUL, JUST IN CASE.

AS A BUYER OF INVESTMENT PROPERTY, IT IS IMPORTANT TO HOOK UP WITH A REAL ESTATE AGENT WHO DOES A LOT OF INVESTMENT WORK. THIS PERSON WILL DO MUCH OF THE PRELIMINARY WORK FOR YOU AND GIVE YOU INSIGHT INTO WHAT KIND OF DEAL IT IS FOR THE AREA, WHAT WILL NEED IMMEDIATE ATTENTION, AND WHAT RENTS ARE IN THE AREA. SINCE, IN MOST CASES, THE SELLER PAYS THE COMMISSION, YOU WOULD NOT BE

INCONVENIENCING AN AGENT BY ASKING FOR HIS/HER ASSISTANCE IN FINDING EITHER ASSUMABLE OR "FREE AND CLEAR" PROPERTIES FOR YOUR CONSIDERATION.

WE HAVE TO UNDERSTAND JUST WHAT GOES INTO DECISION MAKING AND HOW WE CAN ARRIVE AT FIRM DECISIONS THAT WE WILL BACK UP WITH CONVICTION. TO STAY WITH A POSITION THROUGH A DIFFICULT NEGOTIATION REQUIRES ADEQUATE DECISION MAKING CAPABILITIES AND, MOST IMPORTANTLY, BELIEF IN OUR PERSONAL ABILITY TO MAKE AN INTELLIGENT, INFORMED DECISION AND STAND BY IT. THIS, BY THE WAY, IS A MAJOR PROBLEM NOT ONLY FOR INDIVIDUALS TODAY, BUT FOR POLITICIANS, BUSINESSMEN AND POLICY MAKERS IN EVERY ARENA. POLITICIANS AND SPOKESPEOPLE FOR COMPANIES PANDER TO EVERY LOCAL GROUP THAT MAKES NOISE AND EVERY POLL THAT COMES DOWN THE PIKE. AFTER MAKING A DECISION, VERY FEW POLITICIANS WILL STAND BY IT ONCE THE NOISE STARTS. WE, AS INDIVIDUALS, ARE ALSO GUILTY OF THIS. WE ARE AFRAID TO WALK-AWAY FROM A NEGOTIATION THAT WILL NOT REMOTELY MEET OUR NEEDS. WE ARE AFRAID TO

HURT SOMEONE'S FEELINGS, AND WE ALMOST ALWAYS PAY THE ASKING PRICE AND THEN COMPLAIN THAT THINGS COST TOO MUCH.

IN DECISION MAKING OF ANY TYPE IT IS OFTEN HELPFUL TO SIT DOWN WITH PENCIL AND PAPER AND MAKE TWO COLUMNS, A PLUS COLUMN AND A NEGATIVE COLUMN. SINCE NO DECISION IS A PERFECT DECISION, THERE ARE GOING TO BE PLUSES AND MINUSES REGARDLESS. THEN LIST ON THE SIDE ALL OF THE CRITERION THAT WENT INTO YOUR DECISION; CONDITION OF PROPERTY, NEED FOR CASH FLOW, TAX BREAKS, ETC. IF, IN THE END, THE PLUSES OUTWEIGH THE MINUSES, GO FOR IT. MAKE AN OFFER ON THE PROPERTY. THE MAIN PHENOMENON HOLDING US BACK FROM BECOMING WHAT WE WANT IS NOT LACK OF SKILL OR DESIRE OR TALENT, IT IS FEAR AND FEAR ALONE, AS FRANKLIN D. ROOSEVELT SAID.

WHY IS THERE SO MUCH FEAR IN MAKING LARGE PURCHASES AND LARGE DECISIONS? I FEEL THAT MOST OF US REALLY DON'T TRUST OUR DECISION MAKING ABILITIES AND REALLY DOUBT OUR ACTUAL CONVICTION TOWARD A CERTAIN FEELING OR PROJECT. WE MAKE DECISIONS WITH OUR HEARTS

AND NOT OUR MINDS. WHY DO YOU THINK THERE IS OVER A 50% DIVORCE RATE IN THIS COUNTRY? IT IS SIMPLY BECAUSE COUPLES WHO BECOME INVOLVED LET THEIR EMOTIONS TAKE OVER AND THEN ARE AFRAID TO HURT THE OTHER PARTY SHOULD FEELINGS CHANGE THAT WEREN'T REAL IN THE FIRST PLACE. I HAVE ALWAYS SAID THAT PEOPLE PUT MORE THOUGHT AND EXAMINATION INTO BUYING A CAR THAN THEY DO IN EXAMINING A POTENTIAL SPOUSE. DO WE FIND OUT WHAT PLANS OUR FIANCEE HAS FOR WORK, SCHOOL, CHILDREN, ETC., BEFORE THAT BIG DAY? HECK, NO, WE CAN WORK IT OUT, MOST OF US SAY. DO YOUR CHECKLIST BEFORE YOU SAY YES. WILL HE BE A GOOD FATHER? DOES HE/SHE MAKE ENOUGH INCOME TO HELP YOU LIVE LIKE YOU WANT TO AND WHERE YOU WANT TO? DO WE NEED TWO INCOMES TO PAY THIS MORTGAGE FOR THE LONG TERM OR NOT? IF SO, AND SITUATIONS CHANGE, YOU MAY HAVE TO SELL THE HOME OF YOUR EXPENSIVE DREAMS. BEWARE OF BECOMING HOUSE POOR JUST TO IMPRESS THE RELATIVES. THESE QUESTIONS ARE JUST AS IMPORTANT AS "DOES HE LOVE ME, OR DOES SHE LOVE ME?" MOST PEOPLE THINK THAT LOVE IS AN EXCLUSIVE ONCE IN A

LIFETIME HAPPENING THAT WILL NEVER COME AGAIN. THE TRUTH IS THAT MANY OF US HAVE FALLEN IN LOVE MANY TIMES AND THAT IS NATURAL. ISN'T TIMING IMPORTANT IN DETERMINING WHO WE MARRY? THE MORE EXPERIENCE A PERSON HAS WITH A PARTICULAR SUBJECT, WHETHER REAL ESTATE OR SCIENCE, ETC., THE MORE LIKELY ANY DECISION WILL BE CORRECT BECAUSE MORE BASES WILL BE COVERED IN THE DECISION PROCESS ITSELF. EXPERIENCE, HOWEVER, CANNOT BE CREATED OVERNIGHT AND INVOLVES MORE FAILURE THAN SUCCESS.

HOW IN THE WORLD DO WE GAIN EXPERIENCE THROUGH FAILURE IF WE ARE SO PARALYZED BY FEAR THAT WE DON'T EVEN TRY. I HAVE TWO POSTERS IN MY OFFICE THAT SAY, "YOU NEVER FAIL UNTIL YOU STOP TRYING, " AND "TO TRY AND FAIL IS BETTER THAN NEVER HAVING TRIED AT ALL." I HAVE FRIENDS IN THEIR 40's WHO DON'T OWN HOMES AND ARE NOT MARRIED AND CAN'T STAY WITH A PERSON IN A RELATIONSHIP FOR MORE THAN A MONTH. I HAVE SPOKEN TO THEM ABOUT THIS OBVIOUSLY LONELY PHENOMENON AND WHAT IT BOILS DOWN TO IS THAT THEY ARE AFRAID OF GETTING BURNED

Buyers and Sellers Real Estate Handbook

AND OF NOT FINDING THE "PERFECT" PERSON OR "PERFECT" HOUSING SITUATION. THEY ARE PARALYZED INTO LONELINESS BY FEAR AND AN IMAGINED NEED FOR PERFECTION.

WE ARE ONLY ON THIS EARTH A SHORT TIME AND LIKE A FOOTBALL GAME, THE WHISTLE WILL BLOW. TO LIVE A FULL LIFE, WE MUST TRY TO EXPERIENCE ALL THAT WE CAN AND WANT TO, REGARDLESS OF WHETHER WE MAY OR MAY NOT FAIL. YOU WILL BE HAPPIER AT 70 WHEN YOU'RE' ROCKING IN YOUR CHAIR KNOWING THAT YOU TRIED TO OWN PROPERTY RATHER THAN BEING FRUSTRATED AT NEVER HAVING THE COURAGE TO ACT AND NEVER KNOWING WHAT POTENTIAL YOU MIGHT HAVE HAD. OWNING INCOME PROPERTY IS NOT FOR EVERYONE. THERE IS A LOT OF WORK AND EXPENSE INVOLVED IN OWNING ANY TYPE OF PROPERTY. REAL ESTATE, HOWEVER, CONTINUES TO BE A GOOD INVESTMENT, BUT ONLY FOR THE LONG TERM. IF YOU BUY WITH THAT IN MIND, YOU WILL BE BETTER OFF. REMEMBER, THERE IS NO PROBLEM THAT CAN'T BE WORKED OUT IF WE ONLY ASK FOR HELP. AND, REMEMBER, WHEN FACING THAT PROBLEM TO SAY OVER AND OVER AGAIN, "THIS TOO SHALL PASS."

Alan Ray Hoxie

NEGOTIATING IS JUST LIKE PLAYING POKER, YOU'VE GOT TO REMAIN CALM AND STOIC EVEN WHEN YOU'VE GOT FOUR ACES. IF YOU'VE NEGOTIATED A GOOD DEAL FOR YOU, WAIT UNTIL YOU GET HOME BEFORE YOU CELEBRATE. I DON'T CELEBRATE ANYMORE SINCE I KNOW THAT EVEN IF I GET A GOOD DEAL ON A PROPERTY WITH A DECENT CASH FLOW, THERE WILL BE TENANT PROBLEMS AND REPAIRS DOWN THE ROAD, BUT IF MAKING MONEY WERE EASY, EVERYONE WOULD HAVE IT. "NO PAIN, NO GAIN." I HAVE NEVER SEEN AN INVESTOR WITHOUT AN OUTGOING PERSONALITY SO IF YOU,RE NOT ONE WHO WANTS TO MEET STRANGERS, INVEST IN C.D.'S AND STOCKS. A GOOD INVESTOR WILL TALK TO EVERYONE TO ARRIVE AT THE BEST DEAL FOR HIMSELF. HE WILL INTERACT WITH OTHER INVESTORS TO SEE IF HE IS GETTING A GOOD DEAL. HE WILL CALL TO CHECK FOR CODE VIOLATIONS AND PERHAPS CALL HIS ACCOUNTANT TO GO OVER TAX CONSEQUENCES OF HIS PROPOSED DEAL. YOU CANNOT EXIST IN A VACUUM AND BE SUCCESSFUL IN REAL ESTATE. YOU'VE GOT TO ESTABLISH A "FEEL FOR THE DEAL" AND IT ONLY COMES THROUGH DIRECT PERSONAL INVOLVEMENT AND EXPERIENCE.

IS IT SCARY AT FIRST AND RISKY, YOU BET IT IS, BUT SO IS ROBBING A BANK. ONE IS LEGAL, ONE IS NOT. IF ONE FAILS, YOU WON'T BE LOCKED UP, IF THE OTHER FAILS, WELL ... THERE IS NO QUICK, EASY, LEGAL WAY TO MAKE MONEY, EXCEPT FOR SELLING VIA MAIL ORDER OVER MASS MEDIA. SO START THINKING EXPERIENCE, NOT GET RICH QUICK.

THE BEST FEELING YOU WILL EVER HAVE IS THE FEELING OF FREEDOM WHICH COMES FROM KNOWING THAT YOU HAVE A MONTHLY CASH FLOW ENOUGH TO LIVE ON, REGARDLESS OF WHAT YOUR COMPANY OR YOUR BOSS DOES. MY BEST FRIEND WAS LET GO AFTER TEN YEARS AT A MAJOR UNIVERSITY, MAKING $70,000 PER YEAR. WHERE'S HE GOING NOW? HE GOT SOME PENSION MONEY, AND HE WANTS NOW TO LOOK FOR PROPERTY TO ESTABLISH A REGULAR CASH FLOW. THIS WILL TAKE TIME, OF COURSE. WHEN YOUR COMPANY DECIDES TO CUT COSTS AND LOOKS TO THE CHEAP LABOR OVERSEAS AND IN MEXICO, WHERE WILL YOU BE? WILL YOU HAVE AT LEAST $1,000 A MONTHLY CASH FLOW WHEN THEY LOCK AND CHAIN THE DOORS, OR WILL YOU BE STANDING IN THE UNEMPLOYMENT LINE WAITING FOR THE BENEFITS TO RUN OUT? THERE

ARE NO MORE AMERICAN COMPANIES, ONLY COMPANIES THAT DO BUSINESS IN AMERICA. NATIONALISM HAS GIVEN WAY TO PRIDE IN EARNINGS AND DIVIDENDS, A GLOBAL UNDERSTANDING. TO YOUR COMPANY, YOU ARE JUST A NUMBER TO BE ADDED, SUBTRACTED OR ELIMINATED. IT IS TIME TO TAKE CARE OF NUMBER ONE. THERE WON'T ALWAYS BE SOMEONE TO HAND YOU A CHECK. IF YOU'RE A UNION MEMBER AND GO ON STRIKE, I'LL BET A LITTLE RENTAL INCOME WOULD HELP EASE THE PAIN. BECOME AN ACTIVE PLAYER IN LIFE AND NOT JUST A BYSTANDER. YOU WON'T GET A SECOND CHANCE.

KEEP A POSITIVE ATTITUDE. DON'T LET BANKS OR TENANTS DRIVE YOU CRAZY. DON'T PANIC, AND REMEMBER, * "A JOURNEY OF 1,000 MILES BEGINS WITH A SINGLE STEP." MAKE THAT STEP.

THERE ARE MANY WAYS TO BUY REAL ESTATE, AND WE HAVE GONE OVER SOME OF THEM. WHEN YOU BUY YOUR FIRST HOME, REMEMBER, BANKS ARE NOT THE ONLY WAY TO GO. OWNER HELD MORTGAGES ARE ON THE RISE, SO LOOK FOR THEM. ESTABLISH A HOME EQUITY LINE ONCE YOU BUY SO THAT YOU WILL BE ABLE TO TAP THAT EQUITY

WITHOUT HAVING TO PERSONALLY BORROW OR REFINANCE. THIS WILL ALLOW YOU TO BUY A SECOND HOME FOR INVESTMENT, IF YOU CHOOSE THAT ROUTE. ASK RELATIVES OR BUSINESS ASSOCIATES TO BE YOUR PARTNERS, ESPECIALLY IF YOU ARE CASH POOR. HOOK UP WITH A REALTOR WHO CAN GIVE YOU INFORMATION ON HUD FORECLOSURES AND TAX DELINQUENT PROPERTIES IN YOUR MUNICIPALITY. DO AS MUCH WORK AS YOU CAN YOURSELF TO INCREASE YOUR EQUITY WITHOUT MUCH OUT OF POCKET OUTLAY. BEFRIEND TRADES PEOPLE WHO CAN DO WORK FOR YOU AT A REDUCED RATE AFTER THEIR NORMAL WORK DAY, OR LOOK FOR RETIREES INTERESTED. WHEN BUYING LAND OR VACATION PROPERTY, REMEMBER TO CHECK TO SEE THAT THE ZONING IS APPROPRIATE FOR YOUR INTENDED USE.

THREE ARE MANY REAL ESTATE COURSES AVAILABLE THROUGH LOCAL BOARDS OF REALTORS AND COMMUNITY COLLEGES. THE MAKE UP OF MANY OF THESE CLASSES ARE OF THOSE INTERESTED IN OBTAINING A SALES LICENSE AND ALSO INTERESTED IN INVESTING IN REAL ESTATE PROJECTS. REAL ESTATE IS A WIDE OPEN, LITTLE REGULATED FIELD,

AND THERE IS A LOT OF KNOWLEDGE THAT HAS TO BE GAINED TO SUCCESSFULLY OBTAIN SUFFICIENT CASH FLOW TO BECOME FINANCIALLY INDEPENDENT, ATTEND SEMINARS AND RAID THE LOCAL LIBRARY FOR BOOKS AND TAPES ON REAL ESTATE AND THE ART OF NEGOTIATING. YOU,VE GOT TO, HOWEVER, GET INTO THE MIX. IF YOU SIT AROUND WORRYING ABOUT LOSING MONEY, YOU WILL NEVER GAIN ANY. THOSE WHO TAKE RISKS ARE REWARDED, NOT THOSE WHO ONLY DREAM. THE MORE CONFIDENCE YOU GAIN, THE EASIER IT WILL BE TO WORK WITH TENANTS AND BANKS AND SELLERS. BE PATIENT. YOU WILL KNOW BY COMPARABLE EXAMINATION IF YOU ARE PAYING THE RIGHT PRICE FOR A PROPERTY.

UNFORTUNATELY, REAL ESTATE PRINCIPLES ARE NOT TAUGHT IN HIGH SCHOOL AND ARE RARELY OFFERED IN COLLEGES. YOU WILL HAVE TO PURSUE YOUR OWN EDUCATION IN THIS MOST COMMON AREA OF INVESTMENT. MOST LAWYERS MAKE A GOOD AMOUNT OF THEIR INCOME THROUGH REAL ESTATE TRANSACTIONS; YET, THERE ARE FEW COURSES AVAILABLE THROUGH TRADITIONAL INSTITUTIONAL LEARNING.

CONCLUSION

IF YOU HAVE PURCHASED THIS BOOK, YOU HAVE AN ABOVE~AVERAGE INTEREST IN THE SUBJECT, SO GET ON WITH IT. PUT OUT ALL KINDS OF FEELERS THAT LET PEOPLE KNOW THAT YOU ARE INTERESTED IN BUYING AND/OR EVENTUALLY SELLING. EVEN WITH $500 POSITIVE CASH FLOW COMING IN EACH MONTH, YOU MAY BE ABLE TO WITHSTAND THAT LAYOFF OR STRIKE OR PLANT SHUTDOWN UNTIL BETTER TIMES ARE ON THE HORIZON. YOU ARE A NUMBER ON A BALANCE SHEET TO YOUR COMPANY, BUT YOU CAN PERSONALIZE AND INDIVIDUALIZE YOUR INCOME THROUGH REAL ESTATE PURCHASE AND LEVERAGE POWER. BEING ON THE LANDLORD SIDE OF A RENTAL AGREEMENT IS A LOT MORE REWARDING THAN BEING ON THE OTHER SIDE.

REMEMBER, REAL ESTATE INVESTING IS FOR THE LONG HAUL, NOT FOR A QUICK FINANCIAL FIX. EVERY DAY YOUR PROPERTY SITS THERE, HOWEVER, IT IS EARNING MONEY FOR YOU. THERE IS ABUNDANT TALK OF HOW SOCIAL SECURITY WILL BE OUT OF BUSINESS BY 2010. NOW IS THE TIME TO TAKE YOUR FINANCIAL LIFE IN YOUR OWN HANDS. INVESTING AT

THE RIGHT TIME AT THE RIGHT PRICE. HOW IS THAT KNOWLEDGE OBTAINED? TIME AND EXPERIENCE ONLY. TAKE THE TIME TO GAIN THE EXPERIENCE.

IN EVERY CITY AND COUNTY OF THE COUNTRY THERE ARE NEIGHBORHOOD AND RURAL PRESERVATION COMPANIES. THESE ARE NOT-FOR-PROFIT ORGANIZATIONS FUNDED BY STATE GOVERNMENTS WHOSE OBJECTIVE IT IS, TO HELP PEOPLE OF MODERATE TO LOW INCOME PURCHASE AND REHABILITATE HOUSING. CALL YOUR STATE HOUSING DEPT. FOR A LISTING OF THESE COMPANIES NEAR YOU. YOU MAY VERY WELL QUALIFY BECAUSE THESE RATIOS TAKE INTO CONSIDERATION DEBT LOAD WHICH IN MOST CASES IS QUITE HIGH. THERE ARE SIGNIFICANT BENEFITS IF YOU DO QUALIFY, DOES 20,000$ FOR A DOWN PAYMENT SOUND GOOD? HAPPENS ALL THE TIME. THERE ARE OPPORTUNITIES FOR SUBSIDIZED AND LOW INTEREST MORTGAGES AS WELL AS MONEY FOR REPAIRS. THE AMOUNT OF MONEY THE FEDERAL GOVERNMENT HAS COMMITTED TO THE STATES WILL BE GOING UP FOR THE NEXT 3 YRS, IN THE AREA OF HOUSING. DEVELOPING AFFORDABLE HOUSING WILL BECOME A PRIORITY IN THE NEXT 5 YRS, SO DON'T BE LEFT OUT.

THERE IS MONEY AVAILABLE THROUGH THESE CHANNELS TO BUY AND DEVELOP MULTI-FAMILY UNITS FOR INVESTORS AS WELL. CALL THESE GROUPS AND SEE IF YOU FIT INTO ANY OF THEIR PROGRAMS. THE DEVELOPMENT OF AFFORDABLE HOUSING IS A PRIORITY IN EVERY STATE. TAKE ADVANTAGE OF THIS FUNDING TO JUMP START YOUR "HOMEOWNERSHIP EXPERIENCE" GOD BLESS, GO TO IT!

THANKS FOR YOUR INTEREST,

ALAN RAY HOXIE

QUESTIONS / COMMENTS   ahoxie@twcny.rr.com